C000280054

NATIONALISM

NATIONALISM

ERNEST GELLNER

Weidenfeld & Nicolson
LONDON

First published in Great Britain in 1997 by Weidenfeld & Nicolson

© 1997 Ernest Gellner

The moral right of Ernest Gellner to be identified as the author
of this work has been asserted in accordance with
the Copyright, Designs and Patents Act of 1988

All rights reserved. No part of this publication may be
reproduced, stored in a retrieval system, or transmitted, in
any form or by any means, electronic, mechanical
photocopying, recording or otherwise, without the prior
permission of both the copyright owner and the above publisher
of this book

A CIP catalogue record for this book
is available from the British Library

ISBN 0 297 81612 8

Typeset by Selwood Systems, Midsomer Norton

Set in Janson
Printed in Great Britain by Butler & Tanner Ltd,
Frome and London

Weidenfeld & Nicolson

The Orion Publishing Group
Orion House
5 Upper Saint Martin's Lane
London WC2H 9EA

⹀CONTENTS

⇥PREFACE

In the summer of 1995, just months before his death, my father was working on two books. One you now hold in your hands; the final version was dated 25 August. The other will be published as *Language and Solitude: Wittgenstein, Malinowski and the Habsburg Dilemma*. Of the two, *Nationalism* was the more nearly finished; it was only necessary to add missing quotations and references, correct various typographical errors, and smooth out a few stylistic problems.

The earliest version of my father's theory of nationalism appeared as chapter 7 of *Thought and Change* (Weidenfeld and Nicolson, 1964). He was stimulated to work out a theory, as he records here, by his encounter with Elie Kedourie, one of his colleagues at the LSE, and Kedourie's book *Nationalism* (first edition, 1960). He later reworked his theory and expanded it to book length as *Nations and Nationalism* (Blackwell, 1983). Somewhat to his surprise, this was his best-selling and most translated book, more so than the fullest exposition of his philosophical position (*Legitimation of Belief*, Cambridge University Press, 1975) or his overview of human history (*Plough, Sword and Book*, Collins Harvill, 1988). The popularity of the book on nationalism reflected, it is now clear, the resurgence of interest in the topic on a worldwide scale. Nationalism as a subject was to take up more and more of his time, especially when he moved, after retiring from the University of Cambridge, to the Central European University in Prague where he founded a Centre for the Study of Nationalism. Some of his essays on nationalist thinkers and on other theorists of nationalism, mostly dating from this period, are collected in *Encounters with Nationalism* (Blackwell, 1995). The present book comes, then, at the end of a lifetime's research and reflection on nationalism and related subjects. But it is far from being based merely on cloistered academic reading.

It was my father's personal experience of the Prague of his youth which convinced him that Kedourie's intellectualist theory of nationalism was misleading. Nationalism is not just an erroneous theory that can be disproved and discarded: it was and is an inevitable part of the modern world. Prague in the 1930s was a multicultural and highly cosmopolitan city. The two leading and competing cultures were Czech and German, and there were two universities, one German-speaking, the other Czech-speaking. Both his parents, Rudolf Gellner and Anna Fantl, came from secularised Jewish families. He spoke German with his parents, Czech with his sister and friends, and he learned English after he was sent to the Prague English Grammar School. Rudolf's eldest sister, Hedwig, was an active Zionist, but Rudolf, like many Prague Jews, tended to identify with the Czechs, even though Czech was a language he had to learn as an adult after the creation of the Czechoslovak state in 1918. In the late 1930s, when the Nazi threat became obvious, Rudolf visited London two or three times to prepare the family's flight from Prague, because another of his sisters was married to an Englishman. My father, his sister and mother were permitted to cross Germany by train in April 1939 after the Nazi invasion of Czechoslovakia. His father had to escape with a friend via Poland and Sweden. Not all their relatives managed to escape in time.

These circumstances taught my father the contingent nature of nationalism: nations are not given, but are created by states and by nationalists. Individuals often have to choose between several competing nationalisms. At the same time he saw, in contrast to Kedourie, that nationalism in some form or other is the inevitable destiny of the modern world.

A criticism that is frequently made against my father's theory is that it is 'reductive' and ignores, or fails to appreciate, the feelings that nationalism engenders. In reply to this, he wrote:

I *am* deeply sensitive to the spell of nationalism. I can play about thirty Bohemian folk songs (or songs presented as such in my youth) on my mouth-organ. My oldest friend, whom I have known since the age of three or four and who is Czech and a patriot, cannot bear to hear me play them because he says I do it in such a schmaltzy way, 'crying into the mouth-organ'. I do not think I could have written the book on nationalism which I did write, were I not capable of crying, with the help of a little alcohol, over folk songs, which happen to be my favourite form of music.[1]

Of course, that preference for Czech folk songs did not make him into a Czech nationalist, and it was certainly part of his theory that nationalists rarely have much insight into the roots of nationalism as such. The point is not merely to represent nationalist feelings, but to *explain* them.

Among observers of nationalism, there has, understandably, been much anguish at the violent extremes to which it sometimes leads. While fully aware of these extremes, as this book makes clear, my father did not make them the exclusive focus of his attention. In a discussion with Jacques Rupnik and others, he declared himself to be slightly more optimistic than many writers: he hoped for an 'unholy alliance' of consumerism and moderate, non-territorial nationalism. He also remarked that he would like to see a federal Europe which would be able to impose its authority in order to prevent ecological or terrorist disaster, as well as

[1] Pp. 624–5 of 'Reply to Critics' in J. A. Hall and I. Jarvie eds *The Social Philosophy of Ernest Gellner* (Poznan Studies in the Philosophy of the Sciences and the Humanities 48) (Amsterdam/Atlanta, GA: Rodopi, 1996). Cf. J. Hall ed. *The State of the Nation: Ernest Gellner and the Theory of Nationalism* (Cambridge University Press, forthcoming).

drug- and arms-trafficking – but it should be a Europe which retained its cultural and territorial pluralism.[2]

The present short book is his last word on the subject of nationalism. It also represents his most mature analysis, incorporating as it does his theories of 'time zones' and historical stages, as well as situating his own position in relation to the division conventionally made in discussions of nationalism between primordialists and modernists. It so happens that the last time I saw my father was on 24 October 1995 at a debate with Anthony Smith at Warwick University, where he gave a witty rendition of his ideas on this question, summed up in chapter 15 below called 'Do nations have navels?'.

David N. Gellner,
Brunel University,
London

[2] Pp. 281–2 and pp. 262–3 of 'Conclusion' in J. Rupnik ed. *Le Déchirement des Nations* (Paris: Seuil, 1995).

ONE

Culture and power

Men have always been endowed with culture: a shared style of expression in words, facial expression, body language, style of clothing, preparation and consumption of food, and so forth. Culture is not identical among all men: cultural diversity is one of the central features of human life.

The importance of culture distinguishes men from other species. Culture may not be totally absent in the animal world: traits may on occasion be found in animal groups which are transmitted from one generation to the next, not genetically, but socially. Such a trait then distinguishes a given group from other groups which may be genetically indistinguishable from it. But although culture in this crucial sense – patterns of conduct transmitted through emulation, rather than by the interaction of genetic endowment with the environment – does occur in small doses among some animals, its importance and pervasiveness are simply not comparable with the culture found among humans.

The fact that we are capable of 'culture' at all no doubt

has a genetic precondition. This genetic predisposition may be identical in all men. Such a view has been argued by Noam Chomsky in connection with the human capacity to acquire language, and if this argument is valid, it may well apply not merely to language in the narrower sense, but to the totality of culture. The presence of 'culture', however, introduces a mode of transmission of traits or activities from generation to generation which is no longer dependent on being inscribed into the genetic constitution of the members of the group. This transmission completely changes the rules of the game: it allows incomparably greater diversity and incomparably faster change. It is only superficially para-doxical that this liberation from genetic constraint itself has a genetic base. A specific genetic base is required before culture is possible: once it is possible, it permits develop-ments unconstrained by the usual rules governing genetic change.

The capacity to acquire culture at all must have a genetic precondition, which may well be identical in all mankind. (Obviously, it *need not* be identical: it could be that two or more quite distinct sets of genetic equipment would, both or all of them, permit the formation of culture. It seems unlikely that this miracle should have occurred independently more than once, but it is not logically excluded.) At the same time, this capacity of ours for acquiring culture does not prejudge just *which* culture it is to be. Cultures vary enormously from one community to another, and they can also change with great rapidity within a single community. Societies have been known, for instance, to change their language by col-lective decision, for political reasons. A certain Himalayan trading community, having come to the conclusion that the future lay with the Hindu Nepalese state and not with the previously prestigious Tibeto-Buddhist culture to the north, decided to switch from its own tribal language to Nepalese and from Buddhism to Hinduism. Cultural traits, though often experienced as given, can be under deliberate control. The laws of cultural transmission, whatever they may be, are clearly very different indeed from those of genetic transmission. Virtually by definition, they permit the retention and transfer of acquired characteristics: you might say that culture *is* the perpetuated, and sometimes transformed and manipulated, bank of acquired traits. The consequences of this for the nature of social life are tremendous: it means that diversity is enormous and that change can be exceedingly rapid.

Human societies are not merely characterised by the possession of culture: they are also endowed with organisation. Human beings in any group are differentiated, at the very least, by age and gender, and usually in other ways as well. A human group is never just a summation of individuals, in which the relations of the individuals to each other are of no account; rather, it is always an association within which members have a social position, which carries with it certain expectations, given rights and duties, privileges and obligations.

These two general characteristics, culture and organisation, are the raw material, so to speak, of all social life. They are the two basic elements of social life. They may not be wholly independent: a culture may be dominated by a certain model of social organisation, or a given form of organisation may require a certain type of culture. For instance, Hinduism is a culture which implies caste organisation; the dominant themes of the culture require that men belong to castes, and that these social categories be defined in terms of purity. Or again, a society committed to egalitarian organisation may proscribe radical cultural differences among its members. For instance, some of the successor states of the Habsburg Empire actually proscribed the use of aristocratic titles. But though these two basic categories of social life may not be wholly distinct, it is nevertheless important to distinguish them. Both culture and organisation are universally present in all social life.

The two basic notions are particularly useful in helping to define the main theme of this book: namely, *nationalism*. Nationalism is a political principle which maintains that similarity of culture is the basic social bond. Whatever principles of authority may exist between people depend for their legitimacy on the fact that the members of the group concerned are of the same culture (or, in nationalist idiom, of the same 'nation'). In its extreme version, similarity of culture becomes both the necessary and the sufficient condition of legitimate membership: *only* members of the appropriate culture may join the unit in question, and *all of them* must do so. The aspirations of extreme nationalists are thwarted if their nation-state fails to assemble all the members of the nation, and if it tolerates a significant number of non-members within its borders, particularly so if they occupy places of importance.

This is the core idea of nationalism. We have in fact temporarily defined 'nation' in terms of shared culture, and this definition may need some refinement and qualifications before it can fit the complexities of the real world; however, it is near enough to be a good initial basis for understanding the phenomenon which concerns us.

Culture and organisation, states and nationalism

Culture and social organisation are universal and perennial. States and nationalisms are not. This is an absolutely central and supremely important fact. No theory which fails to recognise this can hope to do justice to the problem. Nations and nationalist sentiments are not found universally, whereas cultures and organisation are. This enables one to formulate the correct question: just what is it about the constellation of culture and organisation which sometimes, but not always, engenders nationalism?

The trouble is that very many people, notably many of those deeply involved in nationalism, fail to recognise and admit this fact, let alone understand or explain it. The existence of a centralised state is an important part of the background of the nationalist vision of the world. But the state itself is not universally present: there are, for instance, stateless tribal societies, within which order is maintained by the balance of power between tribal segments, rather than by some central agency (which is the mechanism we tend to take for granted). Our initial definition of nationalism made it insist on the linkage of organisation and culture: the legitimate unit was to be one composed of persons of the same culture. This is formally correct, yet it misses out what is perhaps the most emotive element in the nationalist attitude: it not only defines the limits of the unit, but it assumes that the unit has an institutional leadership ('the state'), and its main concern is that the positions in this institutional power centre be manned by members of the 'national' culture, the one which defines the unit. To put it in simple language: no foreigners may rule us! This requirement is indeed already implied by the definition of nationalism, but the intensity with which this particular implication is felt must be noted.

Nationalists and others tend to assume that the state is a universal institution of human society. Some early political theory even made this into a doctrine: no society without order, no order without enforcement, no enforcement without appropriate agencies (the state). But in fact, states are not universal: 'acephalous' societies manage to maintain order without possessing specialised order-enforcing agencies or personnel. Small bands of foragers can hardly be credited with a state, even if they have leaders. Even among quite populous agrarian or pastoral populations, and sometimes even in urban communities, no continuous centralisation of power may exist. Order can be maintained by the internal opposition of sub-groups, or by assemblies which do not in any permanent, institutionalised manner delegate power to specialists. If and in as far as nationalism is quite specially concerned with excluding foreigners from key position in the *state*, the whole problem of nationalism scarcely arises when there is no state, and there are no key positions in it. What needs to be noted, then, is that the problem of nationalism in the main arises only in a world in which states are taken for granted and required, *and this does not apply to all humanity*.

But if states are not universal, still less is nationalism itself universal. It simply is not the case that, at all times and in all places, men wanted the boundaries of social units and of cultures to converge, or to put it in a manner closer to their own style, that they wanted to be among their own kind, excluding 'others'. On the contrary: men very, very often lived in units which violated this principle, and most of the time, this violation was accepted without protest or opposition, indeed without any awareness that a vital, alleged universal principle was being violated. How can the nationalist cope with this fact (for such it is)?

Here begins our sustained insistence on the difference between nationalism as it sees itself, and nationalism as, in our view, it really is. Nationalism does indeed see itself as a universal, perennial and inherently – self-evidently – valid principle. It is, on this view, simply 'natural' that people should wish to live with their own kind, that they should be averse to living with people of a different culture and, above all, that they should resent being governed by them. This is perhaps the commonest of 'theories' of nationalism: in one sense it is barely a theory, because it treats the principle as something inherent in human nature, or the very principles of social organisation, so obvious as not really to require any explanation. It is, on this view, only the absence or violation of the principle which needs to be explained. And, of course, the frequent absence of nationalist turbulence in the human past does indeed provide the nationalist with a problem, with something he needs to explain.

This theory is dangerous not merely because it is false, but, more significantly, because the self-evident status which it ascribes to itself, and which indeed attaches to it, makes those who hold it fail to see that they are holding a theory at all. They do not see that this is something contentious and to be examined, rather than a self-evident category which justifiably pervades all thought about man and society. They think they are simply recognising the obvious; they are not theorising at all. What is not perceived as a contentious theory cannot be corrected. If, on top of all this, it is false, the situation is unfortunate.

Nationalists are in fact aware of the *evidence* which makes some of us contest the universality of nationalist sentiments:

they do know, often with anger, that in many societies and many historical periods, nationalism is conspicuous by its absence. They know it, with great bitterness, especially when it relates to the recent past of their own nation. But they explain it in their own way, and their explanation is contained in what is probably the most commonly used word in the nationalist vocabulary: *awakening*. As the Germans used to say in the days of Nazism, *Deutschland erwache!* ('Germany awake!'). Throughout central and eastern European national-ism, the notion of the 'Awakener' (for instance, *buditel* in Czech) is very extensively used. The root of the word is the same as that which occurs in 'the Buddha', but of course what is at issue here is national, not spiritual awakening. Man needs to be awakened not to the nature of mundane strife and suffering and to the methods available for liberation from it, but to his national identity and the political imperatives implicit in it: the need to protect the national culture by endowing it with its own state-protector, the need to unmask, neutralise and drive out the foreigners who wish to destroy and debase that culture. The Buddha and the *buditel* are both of them eager to awaken us, but their respective conceptions, both of the dormant state and of the reality to be revealed by its termination, are quite different. For those for whom human fulfilment is linked to the attainment of national consciousness, and its successful political expression, national awakening is more important than spiritual awak-ening; indeed, it is a form of spiritual awakening, perhaps its highest form.

The nationalist squares the assumption of the universality of nationalism with its widespread absence in the real world, especially in the past, by claiming that it was there, really, but it was asleep. Our nation was ever there; it is an eternal entity, imperishable, transcending the ephemeral beings and generations in which it is transiently incarnated. The basic building blocks of mankind are nations, and their existence is not a contingent and morally irrelevant fact, but, on the contrary, it is central to human fulfilment. Cultural diversity is our manifest destiny and men reach fulfilment through their distinctive national cultures, not through some blood-less universality. But, though ever-present, nationality in all its cultural idiosyncrasy occasionally becomes dormant; it even goes into a kind of Occultation, into hiding. Its sleep is encouraged, or indeed caused, by its enemies, who benefit by increasing their power. The dormission of nationalism, though not normally referred to by this name, is one of the absolutely central doctrines of nationalism. This is no accident: the doctrine is indispensable. Without it, there would be no way of squaring the natural, self-evident, universal standing attributed to the nationalist principle (which the nationalist passionately upholds), and the frequent and conspicuous historical absence of any real concern with that principle (which is an indisputable fact, and which the dogma of dormission reluctantly and with bitterness recognises, as a surface truth, deplorable and to be corrected with all possible speed).

Necessary or contingent?

If nationalism is universal and perennial, it is, presumably, necessary – inherent in the nature of things, of the human psyche, of human society. This is the vision nationalism has of itself, of its own status: and, very significantly, this status is also often ascribed to it by its enemies. Humanitarian internationalists, who deplore the particularism, exclus-iveness, intolerance, narrowness and brutality of nationalism, nevertheless often concede – with great regret – that these traits are deeply and perhaps universally rooted in the human heart or mind. They see themselves as engaged in a painful, arduous struggle with the atavistic, but therefore all the more powerful, tendencies of the human heart. They strive to overcome these tendencies, but not without recognising their strength and ubiquity. They hope that openness, generosity and universal brotherhood will prevail – but they are deeply troubled by the strength of the contrary trends.

We have indicated our scepticism concerning this alleged

universality of nationalism and national feeling, the vision
of the Manichean struggle between atavistic particularism
and enlightened universalism (a vision *shared* by both sides,
even if they support rival teams in this historical Derby), and
our associated doubts concerning the dormission theory.
That doctrine squares the attribution of ubiquity to nationalism with the indisputable fact of the frequent absence of
nationalism on the historic scene. It complements the heroic
role ascribed by nationalism to Awakeners.

An extreme alternative to the attribution of *necessary*
standing to national sentiment is the very opposite view,
which would treat it as utterly *contingent*, an accidental invention, a by-product of the scribblings of a set of thinkers in
one particular historic situation. This view was powerfully
argued by the late Elie Kedourie, in his book *Nationalism*
(1993, first published 1960). To him I owe my own awakening
from dogmatic slumbers on this point – until I read his book,
I continued to assume, or at least not to criticise with lucidity,
the 'naturalness' view of nationalism. I was proud to claim
Elie Kedourie as a friend, though our positive views on this
point and many others were highly divergent. However, his
negative point – nationalism is neither universal nor necessary – seems to me entirely valid, and his book performed a
most valuable service in making this point manifest for many
of us.

This is probably the right place to make clear the general
position which is being presented. There is, first of all, the
question: is nationalism necessary or contingent? Conventional wisdom, stressed by nationalists themselves but
frequently accepted by their internationalist opponents, is
the former. Kedourie is one of the most incisive and eloquent
of the exponents of the rival view, which would turn nationalism into an ideological accident. The famous opening sen-
tence of his book reads: 'Nationalism is a doctrine invented
in Europe at the beginning of the nineteenth century.'

The present argument denies both these extremes, each
of these polar opposites. Nationalism is neither universal and
necessary nor contingent and accidental, the fruit of idle

pens and gullible readers. It *is* the necessary consequence or correlate of certain social conditions, and these do happen to be *our* conditions, and they are also very widespread, deep and pervasive. So nationalism is not at all accidental: its roots are deep and important, it was indeed our destiny, and not some kind of contingent malady, imposed on us by the scribblers of the late Enlightenment. But, on the other hand, the deep roots which engender it are not universally present, and so nationalism is not the destiny of all men. It is the highly probable destiny of some men, and the unlikely condition of many others. Our task is to single out the differences which separate nationalism-prone from nationalism-resistant humanity. We know, as a highly conspicuous historical fact since the end of the eighteenth-century, that we and an ever-increasing proportion – in the end probably a majority – of mankind have fallen into the former camp.

The fact that its powerful presence in our souls is derived from certain social conditions, however important and widespread, tends to give people the impression that this is somehow a 'reductive' theory, one which 'reduces' national sentiment to the standing of being the emotive manifestation of social concerns. Even people with relatively mild, humane and moderate national sentiments are liable to feel, if not outrage, at least irritation at such a suggestion, which they consider to be demeaning. They *love* their country, their people, their culture. Their love is sincere, deep and disinterested. Indisputably, it may on occasion help them and their fellows to rise to levels of altruism and self-sacrifice of which they would not otherwise be capable, and they resent the theoretical 'reduction' of this noble, selfless, self-denying sentiment to the status of an externalisation of social forces. This resentment is natural and understandable, but it is not justified. A sentiment may be rooted in social conditions and provoked by them: that does not make it insincere, inauthentic or incapable of occasioning heroic self-sacrifice. The explanation to be offered is derogatory only if you insist that your national, patriotic sentiment springs directly, unconditionally, from some innermost psychic springs untainted by the influence of the social environment. (Ironically, this would go against the nationalist insistence on cultural specificity, and would anchor nationalism in something pan-human, transcending all cultures and nations.) If *that* is what you require, then indeed you may find the present theory offensive.

If *any* explanation devalues a sentiment, if, as Immanuel Kant appeared to believe, a moral feeling is valid only if self-wrought and untainted by any causation of any kind, then this complaint may have some merit. But the roots which are credited to nationalist feeling by our argument are neither shallow nor despicable. They may not be universally operative in all men and in all social climes, and indeed they are not, but they are located very deep indeed in the human condition as it is in our age. They go to the very heart of our being and our situation. They are powerful, and they are justifiably powerful. Not all their expressions may be admirable, but in themselves, these roots are both inescapable and not dishonourable. They will be analysed in due course: at this point, suffice it to say that the charge of reductionism (frequently made) is not appropriate. National sentiment can be and often is sincere and profound, and those who find it so in their own breasts should not think that this on its own constitutes a refutation of the present theory. It is nothing of the kind. The intensity and depth of the feeling is not denied, or even spurned: on the contrary, it constitutes one of the key premises of the entire position. It is precisely this which is fully recognised, and it is this which must be explained, and a determined attempt is made to do so. The explanation to be offered may or may not be valid: that is another matter, to be left to the judgement of others. But it is simply not the case that the intensity and genuineness of the feeling of nationalism is denied or ignored. The opposite is the case.

Thus our position on the necessity/contingency issue is in the middle: it denies each of these extremes, and affirms that nationalism is indeed necessary in certain conditions (to be specified), but these conditions themselves are not universal. Our middle-of-the-road position on this issue is related to our rather different kind of stand on another issue: there, we are not in the middle, but at one of the two ends. This concerns the other great issue pervading the debate about nationalism: the opposition of modernists and primordialists. The latter claim ancient origins for nationalism; the former seek its origin in features of the modern world. Our position on this issue is clear: nationalism is rooted in modernity.

THREE

A short history of mankind

We began by saying that the two key notions to be used in the exposition are *culture* and *organisation*. The relationship of these two characters to each other changes radically in the course of human history. There follows a brief sketch of the principal stages of human history, from this viewpoint.

Mankind has passed basically through three stages: foraging, agriculture and scientific/industrial society. The bands or small communities of the foraging age were too small for the issue of nationalism to arise at all. The fusion of groups occasionally led to multiculturalism even in small bands (Claude Lévi-Strauss encountered one such in the Brazilian jungle), and there was frequently such a thing as cultural contact. However, the rudimentary nature of political leadership, and the absence of 'high' (codified, script-linked) culture meant that the problem of the relationship of polity and culture, which is the area in which 'nationalism' arises, simply was not present. When there is neither state nor formal education, the question of which culture is favoured by the state in the educational system hardly arises.

Nationalism does, however, arise for such pre-agrarian societies when they survive into the modern world: their exiguous numbers (compared with agrarian and industrial populations), and the relatively large areas they occupy, mean that they tend to be swamped by alien populations in the areas they consider their home, and incorporated into larger political units dominated by other and much larger ethnic groups. The territories in which they hunted, fished or foraged, being extensive, often contain natural resources. Under modern conditions, they can sometimes make a bid for having some of their rights as the original inhabitants recognised. Sometimes, however, they are brutally pushed aside (the Tuareg, for instance, could hardly affirm any claim to the oil in the Sahara over which they had grazed their camels), and in some horrible cases, attempts are made to exterminate them by disease in the interest of undisturbed exploitation of natural resources. This is an important and contentious area, which concerns both humanitarians eager to prevent exploitation (on occasion, genocide) of weak ethnic groups, and ethnographic antiquarians eager to pre-serve some vestiges of a 'disappearing world'. For all this, however, 'nationalism' in anything like the modern form did not arise for foragers, either during the pre-Neolithic-Revolution period, when all mankind were in this stage, or later, when foragers survived either in isolated parts of the world (e.g. Australia) or on the margins of the agrarian world. It does concern them now. Arctic fisherman or foragers, in both the old and the new worlds, are now organised and attain 'national' consciousness in opposition to (say) Russian or Québecois encroachments.

The agrarian age is different. It witnessed an enormous expansion of human populations, made possible by food production and storage. This in turn made possible an enor-mous increase in the complexity of the division of labour and of social organisation. Apart from the proliferation of economic specialisations (craftsmen and traders being added to agricultural producers), there also emerged the Red and the Black: extensive strata of specialists in coercion and violence, on the one hand, and in ritual, doctrine, salvation, therapy and mediation with the transcendent, on the other. Political centralisation (in other words, the state), though certainly not universal among agrarian populations – some governing themselves through the use of ritually fortified sub-groups, practising a kind of balance of power *inside* society – did, however, become widespread, and probably the most common form of political organisation. The hierarchical organisation of society became common: roughly speaking, one could say that complexity and hierarchy progressed together.

In the agrarian age the state existed, at any rate in a very large proportion of societies, and so did cultural differentiation: hence the question of the relationship of political power to culture *did* arise for agrarian populations. In other words, the problem of nationalism did arise: it would have been perfectly possible for someone to propose the theory that the legitimate political unit is one which embraces all the members, and nothing but the members, of a given culture. In simpler terms – Ruritania for the Ruritanians! Let all the Ruritanians be joined in the sacred fatherland! And let no one other than Ruritanians – bar perhaps a small number of well-behaved visitors who know their place as guests, and who do not occupy key decision-making positions – take up much space in the sacred land of Ruritania.

It would have been *possible* to articulate such a theory: the concepts required for its formulation were present; the problem of the nature of the legitimate political unit and authority, which can engender nationalism as an answer, was not unknown. Once writing came into use, the idea of codifying culture and its rules, and then transmitting these by formal education, was present. So it was possible, conceptually speaking, to be a nationalist. Yet, though nationalists were not wholly absent, they were not conspicuous, let alone predominant. Why so?

Agrarian societies are based on food production and storage, and a relatively stable technology. This is virtually the definition of agrarian society. Within it, apart from the distinction already introduced, between state-endowed and stateless societies, there is also the important distinction between illiterate and script-using societies. The latter, as you might say, are capable of storing not only provisions, but also ideas. Or rather, they are equipped with a specially powerful technique for the storage of ideas. Even without writing, societies can 'freeze' ideas, or at least phrases, by ritual incantations which preserve patterns and make them normative.

The technological stability or stagnation of agrarian society has certain overwhelmingly important implications. It means that no radical improvement in output is conceivable: the only increase possible is one based on increasing the use of one of the available factors of production – land and labour – and this inevitably comes up against the Law of Diminishing Returns. In simpler terms, agrarian society has a kind of limit of possible output put upon it, determined by the (*ex hypothesi*) fixed technology, and the finite local resources amenable to that technology. In simple terms: there is a ceiling on possible production, though not on population growth. These societies are Malthusian. Crucial consequence: the struggle for resources or produce in such a society, between its constituent members or sub-groups, is, inevitably, a zero-sum game. No one can gain without someone else incurring a corresponding loss.

Agrarian societies are *inherently* Malthusian. The requirements of labour and defence power make them value offspring or, at any rate, male offspring; the stability of technology imposes a limit on production. These two factors jointly have the implication which made Malthus famous: the exponential growth of population, jointly with the non-exponential growth (if any) of output, means that the society as a whole is never too far removed from the point when it becomes incapable of feeding all its members, and periodically, as a result of harvest failure or social disruption, it faces famine.

Famine does not strike at random. In agrarian societies,

men starve according to rank. Agrarian society is a food-producing and storing system; the silos or stores are guarded, and the contents are distributed only in accordance with the enforced entitlements of the members. In north Africa, the local name for the state is or was *Makhzen*, a word with the same root as store, magazine. The term is highly suggestive: government is by control of the store; government *is* the control of the store.

In this situation, the correct strategy for any individual or group within society is to be intensely concerned with its own position or rank, within the social order, and *not* with the enhancement of output. It is your social standing, your station and its entitlements, which will determine your fate. Extra output is only likely to attract pillage or taxation. It is pointless. Occasionally, extra output may be hidden and used to enhance its owners' security and prospects. But that is rare. More often, the path leads from power to wealth, rather than from wealth to power. In medieval Spain, a saying affirmed that warfare was a quicker as well as a more honourable route to riches than trade. This point can, all in all, be generalised for most agrarian societies.

This profound and important truth is reflected in the characteristic value system of agrarian societies. Generally speaking, they despise work and value *honour*. What is honour? A touchy sensitivity about one's own status, blended with a cult of aggressiveness and skill in coercion and intimidation. These tend to be the dominant values of the ruling strata of agrarian societies. Generally they constitute a 'nobility', and the term, very characteristically, wobbles between referring to membership of a status group, and possession and display of values summed up as 'honour'. Frequently, these as it were 'red' values are combined, in various ways, with the 'black' values of a clerisy. The coercion which dominates agrarian society requires cohesion, which in turn depends on principles of legitimacy for its operation – you need to know whom to gang up with. Coercion operates best if the gangs of coercers are well defined and cohesive, and if their internal authority structure is clear. The ritual and doctrinal maintenance of these principles of legitimacy of membership and leadership also require specialists – namely, priests or clerics of one kind or another – and in this manner, the Black tend to share power and authority with the Red in the agrarian world. The social philosophy of the eighteenth-century Enlightenment consisted, basically, of a repudiation of this world: notoriously, its ambition was to see the last king throttled with the entrails of the last priest. The Enlightenment correctly characterised the basic features of the world it was rejecting; it was mistaken in thinking that world, and the oppression and superstition it lived by, to be simply the fruit of human stupidity, of lack of 'Enlightenment'. The strangling of monarchs with the guts of clerics, attractive though the picture may be, would not on its own terminate the agrarian world and its system of values and illusions. That system is rooted in the logic of the agrarian world, and not in human stupidity, or at least not in stupidity alone.

The basic circle in which agrarian society is locked, is complete, and it is difficult to see how one could break out of it (in fact, this has happened, though no one is quite sure of how it was done). The agrarian situation dictates certain values which inhibit innovation and productive growth; this entails a zero-sum situation which dictates certain values; that in turn ... There is *no* exit from this circle. (Or, if you like, there is one, but it has only happened once, miraculously.)

What concerns us here are the implications of this for the relationship of organisation and culture. Agrarian society tends to be organised hierarchically, with each stratum, and its members, jealously guarding its standing and its privileges, and eager to differentiate itself from lower strata which would, given the chance, usurp some of its perks. The lowest of the large strata in this society, namely the rustic agricultural producers, is also segregated into local village communities. Mobility between these is restricted, mainly because the agricultural producers are generally tied to the land, formally or informally. It helps to impose discipline and ensure that the available surplus is handed over: it would not help the social order if peasants could wander in pursuit of more benign overlords. In western Europe, the diminution of the rigours of serfdom is attributed to the shortage of labour following the Black Death, which apparently encouraged gentry to behave more leniently to underlings, so as to encourage them to stay.

Agrarian society is generally inegalitarian in its values. It even exaggerates its own inequality and hides such mobility as occurs, just as our society tends to do the exact opposite. A rough law seems to apply to social development: the more complex and 'developed', the more inegalitarian (cf. Lenski 1966: 43). So it goes on, until the coming of modernity, which, for reasons to be discussed, reverses the trend and also, for related reasons, engenders nationalism.

Agrarian society encourages cultural differentiation within itself. Such differentiation greatly helps it in its daily functioning. Agrarian society depends on the maintenance of a complex system of ranks, and it is important that these be both visible and felt, that they be both externalised and internalised. If they are clearly seen in all external aspects of conduct, in dress, commensality, accent, body posture, limits of permissible consumption and so forth, this eliminates ambiguity and thus diminishes friction. If a man's station and its rights and duties become part of his soul, his pride, this, once again, helps maintain social discipline. That great classic of the social theory of agrarian society, Plato's *Republic*, in fact defines morality in these very terms: morality consists of each element in the hierarchical social structure performing its assigned task, and no other.

This leads us to the main generalisation concerning the role of culture in agrarian society: its main function is to reinforce, underwrite, and render visible and authoritative, the hierarchical status system of that social order. (The lateral differences between members of the food-producing stratum have a slightly different role in helping to tie its members to their community.) Note that, if this is the primary role of culture in such a society, it cannot at the same time perform a quite different role: namely, to mark the boundaries of the polity.

This is the basic reason why nationalism – the view that the legitimate political unit is made up of anonymous members of the same culture – cannot easily operate in agrarian society. It is deeply antithetical to its main organising principle, status expressed through culture. It is not mobile and anonymous, but holds its members in their 'places', and the places are highlighted by cultural nuance. Similarly of culture does not constitute a political bond within it: quite often, differences of culture express social complementarity and interdependence. In such circumstances, cultural differences often do create or strengthen political solidarity. The characteristic political unit of the agrarian age is generally either much smaller than the limits of a culture – city-states, village communities, tribal segments – or very much larger: culturally eclectic empires which have no reason whatsoever to limit their expansion when they encounter linguistic or cultural boundaries (of which they may be wholly ignorant, and to which they are indifferent). The most characteristic political unit of the agrarian age tended to make joint use of both these principles: a trans-ethnic empire would be superimposed on sub-ethnic communities, which it used as its local agent, tax-collector and deputy.

The characteristic forms of violence and aggression were *intra-* rather than *inter*-cultural. Feuds occur between clans of the same wider culture, aristocrats in principle fight or duel only with others of the same rank. When violent conflict passes beyond the local group, it is generally indifferent to culture and language, even if no longer contained within their limits. Lines of conflict within peasant populations tend to concern local resources, and consequently, the opponents are frequently of the same culture. There is something odd about the idea that people geographically distant, and with no real shared or opposed interests, should align themselves simply in virtue of shared or distinct accent: that is a modern idea, which is generally absent in the agrarian world. Marxists maintain that conflict 'really' occurs between strata (classes), but though this occurs sometimes, in special circumstances (notably in partially commercialised city-states, whose brilliant literature has disproportionately influenced the European vision of history and so made it Marxism-prone), it is not *generally* true. Marxists could save the theory from the contrary facts only by having their own version of the dormission theory: where nationalists maintain that nations are asleep or somnolent, Marxists make the same claim on behalf of classes. Classes 'in themselves' need to become classes 'for themselves' before the ever latent conflict becomes manifest for those meant to be participants in it. Marxists, like nationalists, saw themselves primarily as Awakeners: they just had a different Sleeping Beauty. Durkheim, who saw differentiation between men to be linked to their social complementarity, and thus being conducive to peace and cohesion rather than to conflict, was closer to the truth than Marx, though he erred in lumping together the complementarity found in advanced agrarian civilisations with that found in industrialism.

In fact, generally speaking, history is the story neither of class nor of national conflict. Men throughout history have fought, loathed and killed each other without too much regard to language, race, ethnicity, creed or colour. They did not discriminate in murder and exploitation. The salience of class and national conflicts, and in particular the super-imposition of class and cultural criteria and their influence on alignments in conflict, is something which arises only in special circumstances, and these do appear to operate in our modern world. The imposition of a (so to speak) abstract categorial principle of conflict, the requirement that contestants should be able to identify themselves as belonging to a general category (e.g. a 'nation'), is something special. On the whole, men have been impartial in their hates.

To say all this is not to say that culture is politically insignificant – though generally it indicates vertical status boundaries, rather than lateral territorial limits. Sometimes culture is almost invisible: some Berber tribes, for instance, possess 'Arab' genealogies linking them to the Middle East and even to Biblical–Koranic legends, without any attempt at explanation of why immigrants from the Near East should have switched to a wholly new language group on arrival in north Africa. The myths which confer identity on lineages are simply not brought into relation with what (to us) is a blatant ethnographic fact. The culture-and-language are almost invisible, or at any rate ignored in the creation of the image which places the group in a wider context, and which may engender, or at least ratify, political loyalties. While this is true in central Morocco, it is significant that the linguistic-cultural boundary (between Berber and Arab dialects) becomes visible in southern Tunisia, where it happens to be linked to religion (the Berber language being associated with the recollection of a past heresy).

At other times, culture, far from being invisible, may be the object of reverence. It could scarcely be denied that the ancient Greeks were cultural chauvinists, acutely aware of their cultural distinctiveness and superiority. This did not, however, engender any aspiration to political unification, which was forcibly imposed by the marginally Hellenic Macedonians. It is possible to seek the origins of nationalism in ancient Israel, where an inherently unique and potentially universal deity had, at least for the time being, a culturally distinct and exclusive clientele (cf. Cruise O'Brien 1988: ch. 1).

Closer to modern times, it has been possible to claim the Hussite proto-Reformation of the fifteenth century for Czech nationalism, though the matter remains highly contentious, if only because the boundary between Hussites and loyal Catholics cut across the linguistic boundary in Bohemia and Moravia. There is no doubt but that certain social features found in the agrarian world – bureaucratic centralisation, whether by the Chinese state or in each of the two halves of the later Roman Empire – can lead to the kind of cultural homogenisation required by nationalism. Bureaucratic centralisation by the Enlightened Despots of the eighteenth century certainly helped prepare the ground for nationalism (Mann 1992). Likewise, 'Protestant-type' religious movements, favouring the universalisation of priesthood and direct access to the deity through scripture, may favour identification with a culture, albeit legitimated by linkage to a faith and a path of salvation. However, these various exceptions remain untypical, and do not refute the generalisation that, by and large, in the agrarian world, cultural similarity is not a political bond, and political bonds do not require cultural similarity. One day, all this was to change.

FOUR

The industrial and industrialising world

In various very fundamental ways, the industrial world in which we live (and much of this applies to the industrial*ising* world) is different from the agrarian one. First of all, industrial civilisation is based on economic (and scientific) growth, rather than on a stable technology. This growth is capable of being faster than population growth and frequently is such, especially as the social consequences of industrialism eventually diminish population growth, sometimes reducing it to zero or a minus quantity. In brief, the industrial world is no longer Malthusian.

One of the industrial world's two main principles of political legitimacy – of the assessment of the acceptability of regimes – is indeed economic growth. (The other principle is *nationalism*, which is our theme.) Regimes are acceptable if they can, over a period, engender growth, and they lose their authority if they do not. What had been called, by Sidney and Beatrice Webb, a 'New Civilisation' collapsed ignominiously, and without the slightest external impulsion or even internal violence, simply because it visibly failed to provide growth. Thus ended the world's first and greatest Cold War in a uniquely and unexpectedly clear manner: it never needed to become hot in order to be terminated, which had been a perfectly reasonable, and exceedingly frightening, expectation.

This modern growth-orientation has one immediate consequence: pervasive social mobility. Throughout history, as societies became larger and more complex – more 'developed' – they also tended to become more inegalitarian. Then, suddenly, with the coming of modernity, this trend is reversed, and we appear to be living in an age of ever increasing equalisation of conditions. Tocqueville even made this into the prime and dominant trend of European history since the Middle Ages. Why this astonishing reversal of direction? Were we converted to the ideal of equality by its luminous attractiveness?

We are not mobile because we are egalitarians, we are egalitarians because we are mobile. The mobility in turn is imposed on us by social circumstance. Growth entails innovation, the use of new techniques, hence the creation of new jobs and the relinquishing of old ones. A society which lives by growth, which bribes its members into acquiescing by giving them a confident and justified expectation of moral improvement, rather than by the old method of terror and superstition, cannot conceivably have a stable occupational structure. This may once have had a certain charm, by allowing people to become habituated to their social station, to identify with it, to love it; but the option is no longer available. With a rapidly changing technology and its associated occupational structure, the latter simply cannot be stable. Hence there is no way of running a modern society with a system of castes or estates. The one attempt to do so openly, in South Africa, also failed ignominiously.

Apart from its instability, a modern occupational structure must, in some measure at least, be meritocratic: it must fill some posts at least in terms of the talents and qualifications of available candidates. The proportion of such qualification-related posts to others is probably much higher in industrial society than in agrarian society, though the matter has not, to my knowledge, been formally documented. The qualifications required for performing adequately as a medieval baron are probably not very great: he needs to ride well, shout, impose his authority, possess some political cunning. Consequently, these positions, provided the recruits are trained long enough, can be filled by any random method, and heredity is the simplest and most widely used one. Feudal society can be inegalitarian in that it turns the dominant warrior stratum into a distinct and hereditary estate. It was not open to haggling: as Tocqueville put it, membership was beyond price.

You simply cannot do this in a modern society for professors of physics. (In the social sciences and humanities, this is not quite so obvious.) Mathematico-physical ability may in fact be more gene-linked than horsemanship (which is probably open to a very broad category of able-bodied person, given the training), but nonetheless, a society which turned its Association of Physics Teachers into a caste would rapidly find itself internationally ostracised, and would find its standards rapidly falling.

Innovation and the talent-specificity of many tasks leads to the replacement of rigidly stratified societies by formally egalitarian ones. The placement of members of lower strata over members of higher strata would lead to constant friction: far better to embrace a theory of a kind of baseline equality. All men are equals: differences linked to their occupancy of posts in given bureaucratic hierarchies, or to their bank balances, do not enter their souls, or not too much, and do not officially turn them into radically different kinds of human being. A man cannot take his professional status with him and invoke it outside the workplace. Status operates in office hours, so to speak.

Modern society is not, of course, egalitarian in the sense that it is free of tremendous differences in wealth and power. It is egalitarian in the sense that the differences are arranged along a kind of continuum, so that there is not, at any one point, a major break, ratified by law, ritual or deep custom. The differences are gradual and continuous, and not hallowed. Where there is a deep chasm, such as the one which threatens to surround an identifiable under-class, this is recognised as a scandal, and one questionably compatible with the principles or the functioning of the society. In other cases, there is the belief in, and in some measure the reality of, significant social mobility.

The mobility and anonymity of modern society are very marked features of it. Members relate to the total society directly, without mediation, rather than by belonging first of all to one of its sub-groups. Associations which exist within the total society, though effective and important, are ephemeral and optional, and have no important legal powers over their members. Adherence is not dictated by birth or fortified by awesome ritual; nor does it commit members to irreversible loyalties.

This characteristic of modern society – anonymity, mobility, atomisation – is complemented by another one which is even more important: the semantic nature of work. In the agrarian world, most men worked with their muscle. In industrial society, physical work is virtually unknown, and there is simply no market for human brawn. What passes for manual work generally presupposes the capacity to read instructions and manuals. The garage mechanic, who may lose social standing because his work involves dirtying his hands, is in fact paid not for the use of his physical strength, but for his understanding and handling of quite complex machinery. In brief, what passes for manual work presupposes a level of literacy and sophistication which must often be well above that of the professional scholar of the agrarian age.

When work is semantic it involves the manipulation of messages and contact with a large number of anonymous, frequently invisible partners, at the other end of telephones and faxes, and so forth. The anonymity and invisibility of the partners in communication has an important consequence: context cannot be used in the determination of meaning. In the stable, intimate, restricted communication of agrarian sub-communities, context – status of the participants, their tone, expression, body-posture – was probably the most important constituent in the determination of meaning. Context was, so to speak, the principal phoneme. Only a small number of specialists – lawyers, theologians, bureaucrats – were able, willing or allowed to take part in context-free communication. For the rest, context was everything. Now, it is eliminated from a large part of the communication process which makes up the working lives of men.

The capacity either to articulate or to comprehend context-free messages is not an easy one to acquire. It requires schooling, prolonged schooling. And modern society, given that work is semantic in this manner, requires *everyone* to possess this skill. It is the first society in history in which literacy is near universal; to put it another way, it is also the first society ever in which a high culture becomes the pervasive culture of the entire society, displacing folk or low culture. This is not due, as some educational enthusiasts might suppose, to a miraculous diffusion of commitment to the finer pleasures of the mind. It is a corollary of the manner in which society functions: precision of articulation, such as enables a message to transmit meaning by its own internal resources, without making use of context – a skill possessed in the past by at most a few specialised scribes – is now a precondition of employability and social participation and acceptability. And the communication must take place not merely in a 'high' (i.e. codified, script-linked, educationally transmitted) code, but in some one definite code, say Mandarin Chinese or Oxford English.

That is all. It is this which explains nationalism: the principle – so strange and eccentric in the age of agrarian cultural diversity and of the 'ethnic' division of labour – that homogeneity of culture is *the* political bond, that mastery of (and, one should add, acceptability in) a given high culture (the one used by the surrounding bureaucracies) is the precondition of political, economic and social citizenship. If you satisfy this condition, you can enjoy your *droit de cité*. If you do not, you must accept second-class and subservient status, or you must assimilate, or migrate, or seek to change the situation through irredentist nationalist activity. This principle does not operate in other social conditions and is not a permanent part of the human psyche or social order; it is not an ideological invention, or a political device at the service of other interests; nor is it the expression of dark, blind, atavistic forces. But it operates powerfully in our type of social condition, it has a strong hold over the hearts and minds of men, and it is not transparent to those under its sway, who generally do not understand its genuine mainsprings.

FIVE

The plurality of melting-pots

The argument has invoked two models or ideal types: an agrarian social order in which differences and nuances of culture underwrite a complex system of statuses, but do not indicate the limits of political units, and another one, in which a mobile anonymous mass of participants share the same 'high' culture, relatively free of internal nuances, but linked to the political boundaries of the unit with which it is identified. This is indeed the basic picture.

A legitimate question may arise at this point: if this is *the* key transition of our age, why do we not see a passage from the many-coloured pattern of agrarian complexity to one single homogeneous world culture? As far as our model is concerned, this would not merely be compatible with it, but would seem to be its most obvious and natural corollary. Not only would it seem to be so: many of the most perceptive commentators of the Great Transformation have anticipated just such a pattern. In fact, this is a point on which liberals and Marxists have agreed, at least in outline. The shared framework of their argument could be presented as a kind of syllogism:

1. Ethnic hostility and separatism require cultural differences, for without them, how could ethnic groups, 'nations', identify themselves and distinguish themselves from their enemies?
2. Industrial social organisation erodes cultural nuances.
3. Therefore, the advancement of industrialism erodes the very basis of nationalism.
4. Therefore, the progress of industrialism means the withering away of nationalism.

The argument is impeccable. Its premises are valid. How can a valid inference from true premises yield a conclusion which appears to be wholly refuted by historical reality?

Though the formal skeleton of the argument is identical in both camps, the details vary as between liberals and Marxists. The two melting-pots are not identical. The liberals place their trust in the market and individualism. An international division of labour, beneficial to all, engenders general prosperity in which individuals seek their privately chosen aims, and the mechanism of the market ensures that the pursuit of private benefit is to the advantage of the totality. Individuals attain their private fulfilment through impersonal co-operation in an economically free society, and have neither need nor inclination to fetishise either society as a whole or ethnic sub-segments of it. On the contrary, their perception of the shared political infrastructure is healthily prosaic: it is a public convenience, not an object of worship. No Divine Kingship for post-Enlightenment Man!

The Marxist vision of the melting-pot is a little less rosy, at least in the short run. The harmony of interests in the market is but an illusion: it hides a deep and insoluble *conflict* of interests. The shared political infrastructure, while it likes to present itself as benign and neutral, is in fact inescapably biased in favour of one section of the population and, to make it worse, a numerically diminishing section: its real concern is the political subjection of the disadvantaged majority. All the same, despite this grim picture, inter-nationalism does emerge, perhaps even more powerfully, being born not of shared advantage but of shared, total and desperate deprivation. An inherently international, nation-less proletariat is stripped not only of all but the most minimal material benefits, but also of any specific culture and conceptual incorporation in society: it is not merely humanity in the raw, it is above all *pure* humanity. As such, it is the proud destiny of the working class to restore mankind to its proper essence, its *Gattungs-Wesen*, its species-essence, the curious Aristotelian notion used by Marx to underwrite and validate his moral vision of Communist Man. A Com-munist social order was valid not merely because it will in any case prevail, but because it permits, and assures, the liberation of the true and essential man inside all of us, that had been so vainly struggling to be let out during all those centuries of class-endowed social formations.

Empirically we now know, as clearly as we know anything, that neither of these visions is valid. Wars did not cease in the twentieth century, notwithstanding the growth of inter-national trade: it was not GATT but MAD, mutually assured destruction, which prevented large-scale wars after 1945. The postulated absence of working-class nationalism is a joke.

We know *that* the single-melting-pot thesis, in either liberal or Marxist form, is false, but it would be interesting to know *why* it is false. After all, it had a very great initial plausibility: there was nothing wrong, as far as one can see, with that syllogism which entailed the demise of nationalism. So?

Cultural nuances in the agrarian world are legion: they are like raindrops in a storm, there is no counting of them. But when they all fall on the ground, they do not, as it were, coagulate into one large all-embracing puddle – which is what the universalists-internationalists of either variety expected – nor do they remain separate: in fact, they aggre-gate into a number of distinct, large, often mutually hostile puddles. The aggregation, the elimination of plurality and nuance anticipated by the internationalists, does indeed take place, but it leaves behind not one large universal culture-puddle, but a whole set of them. Why so?

It might have happened in any case, simply in virtue of the lie of the land, so to speak: while, as both our argument and that of the internationalists maintains, modern conditions are indeed most unfavourable to the preservation of local specificity and village-green cultures, the new homogeneity will emerge around points of attraction, hollows in the ground in terms of our metaphor, and the various hollows may be separated by quite high ridges. Pools will form as drops fall, but, except in the most unlikely case of a totally flat and even surface, more than one pool will form. For 'hollows', read attractive, emulation-inviting cultural models, cultures already equipped with writing and codified norms, and capable of absorbing the previously localised cultural patterns, either by possessing affinity with them, or by persuasively proclaiming their own superiority and authority, or both.

Over and above the fact that the sheer lie of the land, as it were, would have caused the mass of erstwhile cultural nuances to congeal not into a single pool, but into a number of new cultural pools, there is also an additional and weighty factor operating in this direction. The tidal wave of industrialisation or modernisation, and, one should add, the social disturbances it actually projects ahead of itself in advance of its full arrival, does not hit all parts of the world at the same time. On the contrary, the diffusion of industrialism is very uneven, both territorially and in the timing of its impact on various parts of a social structure. Sensibility towards the new order, responsiveness to its opportunities and dangers, depends on location, on pre-existing lines of communication, on economic opportunities, in brief on a host of factors which operate in diverse ways and at diverse speeds. Modernisation is spread out over time, and its beneficiaries and victims meet it at diverse dates.

There is frequently a profound conflict of interest between

early and late entrants. If late entrants can only approach the new order as fellow citizens of more privileged predecessors, who have already eaten the forbidden fruit and have accommodated themselves to it, the latecomers are liable to suffer particularly acute disabilities. If they can distinguish themselves culturally from their exploiters and oppressors, it is very much to their advantage to hive off politically, when the opportunity arises, and to modernise under their own flag, in their own sovereign territory. Here they can protect their development from lethal competition by the more advanced, and here their own dialect is spoken with pride, as the state language, rather than muttered with shame as the badge of backwardness and rusticity. In the new unit, the intellectuals drawn from the cultural zone which is in the process of turning itself into a 'nation', can also monopolise all attractive positions, instead of having to compete with more numerous and well-established members of the group which had been dominant in the previous polity.

This is, in fact, one of the commonest and most typical forms of nationalism: German nationalism began in this spirit, not merely as a Herder-ian protectionism of rustic cultures, but also as a List-ian protection of nascent industries and a new bourgeoisie. Karl Marx thought that the German bourgeoisie had no chance whatsoever of catching up with the British and the French, and ought instead to leap a stage and go straight for the Revolution and the next level of social development, under his inspiration. Friedrich List thought the opposite, and it was his course which was adopted, and it was he who was not merely *listig* (cunning), but also right, as admirably described by Roman Szporluk (1988).

It is not only backward populations which have a clear interest in secession and the creation of a new and rival nation-defining high culture, aspiring to its own state. Economically and educationally privileged, specialised urban populations can survive under the old order, in which, when things go well, they benefit from political protection. The monarch is happy to see economic power concentrated in the hands of an urban, insulated and stigmatised population, debarred from possible political ambition and without military clout: wealth in such hands is far less dangerous to him, if dangerous at all, than similar resources in the hands of men with, say, rustic clients habituated to bearing arms. But come the modern order, this protection falters: the insulation of the stigmatised population becomes harder to maintain and defend, and the bulk of the population is no longer content to stay on the land and keep out of trade. Its jealousy and frustration can be appeased by depriving the erstwhile specialised minority of its monopoly in certain spheres – and of its protection. So, although such urban, commercialised and literate populations are specially equipped to do well out of modernity, at the same time, their position makes it politically exceedingly perilous for them. They are destined for ethnic cleansing. So they too have a powerful interest in creating their own territorial political unit, in which they can see to their own defence. The lack of a land base may make the task difficult, but the motivation is strong and is liable to succeed despite this problem.

In brief: there are very good reasons, over and above the sheer unevenness of terrain and the survival-inertia of major cultural groups (especially when endowed with their own script and the institutions perpetuating their own high culture), which make for the emergence, with industrialism, not of one all-embracing universal culture, but of a whole group of them. The emergence of a single universal culture may yet come: only the future will tell. But for the time being, what we see is the replacement of enormous cultural diversity by a limited number of high cultures with political pretensions. That is the age of nationalism. We might not have anticipated it but, with hindsight, we can understand it.

SIX

Stages of transition

We have put forward two extreme and simple ideal types, one conducive to nationalism, the other averse to it. The two types of society could hardly be more different. It is hard to conceive a direct, immediate, single-step transition from the older form to the contemporary one. This being so, what are the intermediate stages through which a given society is liable to pass on its way from one form to the other?

The stages will not be the same in all places and circumstances, of course. It may, however, be useful initially to construct one series of stages, inspired largely by the central European experience, and only subsequently explore the varieties to which this pattern may be subject under different conditions. The point about the central and central-eastern European experience is that it does indeed begin with an almost ideally pure, non-national political system and it ends with an ideally pure, national political system. The political organisation of central and eastern Europe was originally based on dynasties, religions and territorial institutions, rather than on language and its associated culture, but it ended with the very opposite – in some cases, with political units that have been thoroughly, horrifyingly 'cleansed' ethnically, and so satisfy, to an appalling extent, the requirements of the nationalist political imperative. How did this social order pass from the pre-nationalist to the fully nationalist condition?

Stage 1: The Viennese Situation

The first stage might suitably be called the Viennese situation, in recognition of the Congress held in that city to settle the condition and map of Europe after the Napoleonic wars. The peacemakers, and mapmakers in Vienna went about their task in total disregard of ethnicity. Metternich, Talleyrand and Castlereagh did not commission any teams of ethnographers or linguists to explore the cultural or dialectal map of Europe, so as, in as far as possible, not to offend the sensibilities of the peasants when it came to allocating them to their sovereigns. No such thought crossed their minds, any more than it did the minds of the said peasants. There were other considerations to be borne in mind – dynastic interests, religion, the balance of power, traditional local institutions, rights and privileges, even territorial continuity and compactness perhaps. But the idiom of peasants as a touchstone of political legitimacy or the boundary of realms? The suggestion is laughable.

So Castlereagh, Talleyrand and Metternich did indeed go about their business as if the world had not changed so very much since 1789 or, at any rate, as if the clock could be put back. They could do so without being swamped by protests from the countless varieties of east European Ruritanians, to the effect that their sacred rights were being violated, that their holy fatherland was being torn apart and desecrated. The Ruritanians had not achieved self-consciousness, they had not yet been awakened; they may have been a nation-in-itself, but not, or not yet, a nation-for-itself. There may have been some protests from the Poles, well advanced in the nationalist race, but all in all, the practices of the peace-makers were accepted not merely as inevitable because backed by force, but as somehow in the nature of things. Nationalism did not raise its head, and it did not presume to challenge the verdicts of Europe's betters. It would be unfair to say of them, as it was said of Talleyrand's new Bourbon masters, that they had forgotten nothing and learned nothing. They had learned a certain amount: they had a sense of rational estate management. Discontinuous properties were if possible to be avoided, and so, for instance, the Habsburgs willingly gave up their distant possessions in the Low Countries, so as to be compensated nearer to their Viennese base on the southern side of the Alps. Eastern Europe really emerged rather tidy from the Viennese proceedings, neatly carved up among the Romanovs, Habsburgs and Ottomans.

All the same, whether they liked it or not, the world had changed. They, the rulers themselves, were part and parcel of the changes and were eager to advance some of them, which were conducive to the enhancement of their own wealth and power. They rationalised administration, con-tinuing the work of the pre-Napoleonic Enlightened Despots, and were quite eager to expand education. A cen-tralised orderly bureaucracy, implementing general rules and appointed by the centre, not selected, like some Ottoman pasha, in virtue of their local power base, had to use one language or another to communicate with each other from one end of the empire to the other. It ceased to be the ethnically neutral Latin, and became the ethnically divisive German. This in itself, even if the society governed by the new bureaucracy had not been changing, was bound to have potent nationalist-type implications: when the bureaucracy becomes more pervasive and intrusive, and employs one vernacular, the choice of that language becomes important for people. It becomes very significant for the life prospects of individuals just what that language is, whether they are masters of it, and whether it is easily accessible to them (cf. Mann 1992). Also, liberal and Protestant virtues become fashionable, even among authorities with little sympathy for liberalism or Protestantism as such, because these virtues are politically and economically useful. The Prussians free their peasants not because they are smitten with the pure ideal of liberty, but because they do not wish to be thrashed again as they were at Jena: free peasants, it would appear, fight better than serfs, so we had better liberate our serfs, whether we like it or not. Among the first to toy with what later became the Weber thesis about the role of Protestantism in productivity were those arch-champions of the Counter-Reformation, the Habsburgs, eager to emulate the productivity of the Prods, and reforming their educational system with this end in mind...

To sum up: the political system set up in Vienna in 1815 remains totally, uncompromisingly, non-nationalist in its organising principles. Sicily can be swapped for Sardinia, Lombardy for Belgium, Norway for Finland, without a word being spoken about ethnicity, language or culture. What have these frills to do with politics? As for the subjects or victims of these decisions, no doubt most of them would, had they the eloquence, express themselves in the terms commended by Elie Kedourie near the end of his book on nationalism:

> The only criterion capable of public defence is whether the new rulers are less corrupt and grasping, or more just and merciful, or whether there is no change at all, but the corruption, the greed, and the tyranny merely find victims other than those of the departed rulers. (Kedourie 1993 [1960]: 135)

But for all that, forces were already in operation, had in fact been in operation for some time, which were to ensure that a system based on these principles was unlikely to be stable or remain unchallenged. The nationalist snake may not have been perceived, but it was already in the garden.

Stage 2: The Age of Irredentism

The period during which the snake was present in the garden but remained inconspicuous was not due to last long. The first nationalist rebellion occurred just a few years after the Congress of Vienna.

The first nationalist rising was that of the Greeks, and it would be idle to deny that some of its features present a problem for our theory. Our theory links nationalism to industrialism: but early nineteenth-century Athens or Nauplia (the very first capital of newly independent Greece) bore very little resemblance to Engels' Manchester, and the Morea did not look like the Lancashire dales. Blake would have found no satanic mills in Hellas' sometimes green, but more often arid and stony land. To make things worse, the first Greek rising did not even take place in territory considered Hellenic, whether in antiquity or in modern times, but in what is now Romania, and in territory in which Greeks did not constitute a majority or anything like it, but where, interestingly, they were privileged and powerful intermediaries between the populace and the Muslim overlords. In fact, there is reason to suspect that the original Greek national movement aimed not at a homogeneous modern nation-state, but rather at a reversal of ranks within the then Empire: in brief, to put the clock back and replace the Ottoman Empire by a new Byzantium.

Generally speaking, not merely Greek, but also the other Balkan nationalisms can be seen as constituting a major problem for the theory, given the backwardness of the Balkans by the standards of industrialism and modernity. All one can say on this point is that, in the Balkans, two distinct processes overlapped. One of them is the turbulence which is normal in the agrarian world at the mountain or desert edges of empires, where local groups and chiefs make use of any weakening of the imperial centre to make themselves autonomous or independent. But it so happened, in the Balkans, that the overlords were Muslim and the peripheral wild men were Christians. This, as it were, accidental con-

vergence was liable to endow a peripheral dissidence, practised by tribesmen and bandits, with a kind of doctrinal or
ideological content: the rebels were not just rebels, but men
of a distinct faith and hence culture, and when the confrontation is not merely one between rivals for power and
benefits, but between *kinds* of men, nationalism is approach-
ing. Furthermore, the Christian faith they more or less shared
with the West was a kind of conductor: the Enlightenment
and the Romanticism which followed it were both, so to
speak, heresies within Christendom. Fellow Christians were
highly vulnerable to this infection, whereas Muslims were
much less so: a long-standing, ingrained sense of superiority
towards Christians made them less liable to be attracted by
new ideas within Christianity. They were willing to take over
western artillery techniques without the mathematics and
philosophy linked to them: they could have employed
Descartes the officer without heeding the philosopher.

This conductivity by Christianity of anti-Christian heresies within itself must be part of the explanation of why
Balkan rebels – unlike, say, Berber rebels within another
Muslim empire – were not just rebels, but nationalists as
well. This conductivity must also be part of the reason why
the Romanovs modernised faster than the Ottomans, thereby
creating a messianic intelligentsia whose salvation politics
proved fatal in 1917 – a fate Turkey was spared in as far as the
Young Turks were pragmatists concerned with state power,
not salvation-drunk messianists. Bandit-rebels in Balkan
mountains, knowing themselves to be culturally distinct from
those they were fighting, and moreover linked, by faith or
loss-of-faith, to a new uniquely powerful civilisation, thereby
became ideological bandits: in other words, nationalists. I
am not suggesting that the hide-outs of Balkan guerrillas
contained well-thumbed copies of Diderot and Condorcet;
but, indirectly, these rebels and their poets did absorb and
disseminate western ideas, particularly in the form in which
Romanticism both inverted and continued the Enlightenment.

But no matter: whether or not Balkan nationalists can be

enlisted, by invoking a few *ad hoc* special factors, on the side of the thesis which links nationalism to industrialism (notwithstanding the notorious lack of nineteenth-century Detroits, Ruhrs or Black Countries in the Balkans), the other nationalists who came to disturb the long relative peace between Vienna and the shot at Sarajevo on the whole fit the thesis fairly well. What is to be said of this Age of Irredentism which stretches from Vienna to Versailles?

Leaving aside Italy and Germany (we shall deal with them anon), the interesting thing is that, politically, nationalism did not achieve all that much. The Magyars, it is true, improved their position somewhat in 1867, but most of the Slavs did not. (Of course, within the Habsburg Empire, it was impossible for both Magyars and Slavs to do so, for their claims were mutually incompatible.) It is true that, by 1912, five or six buffer states existed in the Balkans, whether as a result of the weakness of the Ottomans or the strength of nationalism; but on the whole, the handiwork of the peace-makers of Vienna had worn well. Eastern Europe, at any rate, did not (on the political map) look so very different from what had been agreed in 1815. This restored *ancien régime* does not seem to have been all that fragile. It stood the test of time.

But in dramatic, striking contrast to its relative failure to modify the political map, nationalism, during the very same period, scored an overwhelming victory in ideology, in literature. Ignored even more than openly spurned in 1815, by 1914 no one ignored it, and most took it for granted. The illusion of the fundamental, natural, self-evident role of nationality in politics was very well established. Some liked to think of themselves as internationalists rather than nationalists, but the popular appeal of such a view was shown to be insignificant in 1914. Come 1918, the crucial standing of nationalism as a principle of political legitimacy is as self-evident as it had been irrelevant in 1815. The moral victory of the principle was nearly complete: very few dared raise their voices against it.

Stage 3: The Age of Versailles and Wilson

The now so self-evident principle was implemented at Versailles – not, admittedly, with an even hand. In areas of great ethnic complexity such as eastern Europe, there is *no* way of implementing the principle fairly. Demographic, historical, geographic and other principles cut across each other. The appeal to referenda will depend, for the result, on how the electoral districts are drawn. Some principles invoked have a certain charm: the Serbs, for instance, do not constitute a majority in Kosovo, but what rational mind could deny that they cannot separate themselves from the location of their greatest national disaster?

The implementation depended a fair amount on who had been on which side in the war, and on geopolitical accident. The new Czechoslovakia (or the reborn Bohemian state, whichever way you wish to look at it) annexed heavily Magyar areas, a mistake which was to cost the new state dear at Munich, with neither demographic nor historical justification, simply because, strategically, the Danube looks like a kind of Rhine, and it was necessary to have a slice of the Pannonian plain if the internal lines of communication of the new state were not to be arduous and precarious. The Magyars and the Bulgarians were unfortunate not merely in having been on the wrong side, but also in being so located as to engender, almost automatically, an alliance of all their neighbours against them, united in a desire to cut a slice of land.

The particular details of the settlement hardly matter. The overall result was only too clear. The system of states set up at Versailles, in the name of the principle of self-determination, was appallingly fragile and feeble. It collapsed at the first storm. The new states had all the weaknesses of the empires they were replacing: they were minority-haunted, at least as much as the empires, and this was inevitable whichever way the boundaries were drawn, short of ethnic cleansing, which in those backward days was not widely practised. On top of that, the new states were inexperienced, small, weak, greedy and opportunistic. They made hay while the sun shone, and for some reason supposed that the sun would go on shining.

It didn't. Come Adolf and Josef, the system collapsed with humiliating ease. What had been built at Versailles had no stability, no staying power. The states born of the principle of self-determination went down easily to a new empire or empires: some offered token resistance, some none; some joined the new masters with a redirected opportunism. There is only one case of successful resistance: Finland. The application of Wilsonian principles in 1918 did not work; an attempt to apply something similar at the collapse of Yugoslavia has had even more tragic consequences, or rather, consequences which were quicker in coming and required no external assistance. The consequences of a similar application in the ex-USSR are yet to be seen.

Stage 4: Ethnic cleansing

The nationalist principle requires that the political unit and the 'ethnic' one be congruent. In other words, given that ethnicity is basically defined in terms of shared cultures, it demands that everyone, or very nearly everyone, within the political unit be of the same culture, and that all those of the same culture be within the same political unit. Simply put: one culture, one state.

There are various ways of attaining this blessed condition. One of them, itself very fortunate and privileged, is by gradual, slow, organic growth. Ernest Renan defined the modern nation, such as can rightly aspire to its own state, in terms of *oblivion*: the members of the nation, and hence of the state, have simply *forgotten* their diversity of cultural origin. The average Frenchman knows he drinks wine, has a decoration and knows no geography. This is the most popular definition of the typical Frenchman, invoked in France itself. But this typical Frenchman does *not* know whether he or rather his ancestors were Gauls, Bretons, Franks, Burgundians, Romans, Normans or something else. It is this national Cloud of Unknowing, this blessed amnesia, which *makes* France. Renan's contrast was with the Ottoman Empire, not at all a national state, in which, he said, the Arabs, Turks, Greeks, Armenians, Jews and so forth knew then, at the time he was writing, as well as on the first day of the Ottoman conquest, that they were Arabs, Turks, etc. He should really have said that they knew it *better* even than they had at the inception of the empire: at that early period, their general cultural or religious category may well have been obscured by some local communal membership, whereas the Ottomans, by organising the overall society into self-administering ethnic-religious 'millets', made this millet-ethnicity highly visible and significant, and thus obliged people to identify with it.

A thousand years of history of an (on and off) strong state have achieved that blessed oblivion which Renan praised and singled out as the essence of nationhood. He was right: it is the anonymity of the membership, the participation in the total 'nation' *unmediated* by any significant sub-groupings, which is what distinguishes the modern nation.

But the French have been granted a thousand years to achieve this. What of young-nations-in-a-hurry, eager to forge that homogeneous culture-and-state unit, and unable or unwilling to wait for a long, slow process of dissolution and forgetting of differences?

There is one way in which such homogeneity can be achieved with speed, and since the Yugoslav tragedy it has a name: ethnic cleansing. It constitutes stage 4 of the sequence we are spelling out, on the basis largely of central European history. In central Europe, the main age of this process was the 1940s. Wartime secrecy, the racism-and-ruthlessness ideology of the then masters of Europe, and then victors' licence granted by indignation and opportunity after the end of the war, made possible methods of attaining homogeneity – mass murder, forced migration, migration induced by intimidation – which in more normal times men shrink from. These methods were in fact used.

Of course, these methods were not invented in the 1940s.

It had all happened to the Armenians very early; on a more modest scale, some of it happened in the Balkans during and at the end of the Balkan wars; it happened between Greeks and Turks at the beginning of the 1920s; it is happening at present in ex-Yugoslavia and, on a proportionately much smaller scale, in the ex-USSR. But the really outstanding period of this process was the 1940s.

Stage 5: Attenuation of National Feeling

This stage may be part reality, part wish-fulfilment. In advanced industrial society, some processes are set in motion which do, or may, diminish the intensity of ethnic feelings in political life. There is perhaps some measure of truth in the old convergence theory of industrial societies, which claimed that, as time progresses, they all come to resemble each other. The theory was originally formulated in the context of rival capitalist and Communist industrialisms, predicting that the two would assume each other's features. The theory has survived the collapse of Communism and the disappearance of its original motive. It seems to have some measure of validity when the cultural baseline is similar – various European industrialisms come to resemble each other with time – but it is far less clear that a similar convergence operates for, say, east Asian and European industrial societies. The European convergence seems particularly marked, for instance, in the sphere of youth culture: the Soviet Union capitulated to Coca-Cola and to blue jeans long before it surrendered to the market and political pluralism.

In so far as this is true, advanced industrial cultures may come to differ, so to speak, phonetically without differing semantically: different words come to stand for the same concepts. People who 'speak the same language', without literally speaking the same language, may be able to cohabit and communicate even in a mobile society committed to semantic work. Phonetic diversity without semantic diversity may lead to less friction, especially if, for work purposes, people are bilingual, or one language is the idiom of work.

This consideration does not operate, of course, when it comes to the relationship between a host community and labour migrants who 'do not speak the same language' on top of not speaking the same language. The geographic area where diminution of the intensity of ethnic feeling has been observed is western and even parts of central Europe, but this diminution does not apply to culturally distant labour migrants.

Stable government plus affluence and the expectation of growth do jointly militate against extremism. People who may or may not harbour personal ethnic prejudices will not sacrifice their security and comfort for the sake of provoking violent conflict. The danger arises when these conditions fail to apply: for instance, during the collapse of large political units (e.g. the Habsburg, Bolshevik or Yugoslav states). When authority collapses anyway, when no centre is authoritative in virtue of being recognised by most other members of the society, when new authorities need to be created and one selected from among a number of rival pretenders, then – apart from competitive terror (the commonest way of singling out the victor and recipient of new legitimacy) – a good way of recovering social cohesion is through ethnic movements. They can be activated and mobilised more quickly than movements based on more complex considerations: the marks and symbols of ethnic membership are more conspicuous in the modern world than any other. This may be sad, but it is a fact.

Ethnic conflict is frequently about territory. The symbolism of land continues to be potent in the emotional poetry of nationalism. Nevertheless, a great ideological change has come over much of the world since 1945: the brilliant success of the two major defeated nations and the economic malaise of some of the victors have made it plain that what makes you big, important, rich and strong in the modern world is not acreage, but rates of growth. This lesson has sunk in, and is at least a contributory factor to the diminution of nationalist ardour.

These are some of the factors which help to explain the diminution of nationalist virulence in a world in which the basic factors making for nationalism – the semantic nature of work, the dependence of everyone on the mastery of and acceptability in a named high culture: in other words, a 'nation' – continue to operate powerfully. We shall also consider this problem in the context of the question: what made nationalism so very acute during the first half of the twentieth century? This is the obverse of the question: why is it diminishing now (if indeed it is)? Whether nationalism is indeed diminishing is contentious and only time will tell.

SEVEN

The marriage of state and culture

The above five-stage scenario presented one possible sequence, but the world is more varied than that. Even within Europe alone, ignoring the complexities of other cultures, the patterns are more diversified. In fact, in Europe, one can discern three or four time zones, rather like the world maps at airports indicating time differences in various areas. In this case, what concerns us are belts of territory running from north to south, within which the pattern is roughly similar, but which differ from one zone to another.

Zone 1

Let us present the differences in terms of this *marriage* of state and culture. The form this union has taken differs from zone to zone. Proceeding from west to east, against the sun, we have first of all Europe's Atlantic coast and the societies spread out along it.

The crucial fact about this area is that the couple were living together in a kind of customary marriage for ages, long before the Age of Nationalism, and long before the internal logic of modern society decreed that the couple were meant for each other. Some other factors, whatever they may have been, brought the couple together, in a union, or a series of such unions, which when they began were barely noticed and not formally hallowed by the sacred nationalist doctrine.

To put the point non-metaphorically: the strong dynastic states based on Lisbon, Madrid, Paris and London more or less corresponded to cultural-linguistic zones anyway, even before the logic of the situation, or nationalist theory, decreed that such a correlation should obtain. The fit was far from perfect, and there was, of course, a considerable amount of dialectal differentiation within the territory of each state. All the same, these differences were not excessive, and the important cultural differences were to be found more between social strata than between regions. So, when the Age of Nationalism arrived, no great changes were required in this zone. To understand the political map of western Europe, it is still more important to know about the dynastic conflicts of the late seventeenth and eighteenth centuries, to know something of Louis XIV's campaigns, than to be familiar with the ethnographic map of Europe. In this zone, only one major change has occurred on the map as a result of nationalism: the creation of the Republic of Ireland.

This does not mean, of course, that nationalism was absent from the hearts and minds of the members of these cultures which had their roof-state given by history before they ever needed to claim it: and Joan of Arc is often presented, perhaps anachronistically, as an early modern nationalist. But during the post-medieval centuries, these cultures did not need to strive for the creation of their political carapace, they already had it. There were, of course, some smaller cultures located inside their territory which did need to struggle, but the main cultures did not. The political and cultural centralisation inherent in modernity meant that the peasants or the working class needed to be educated, to be taught to 'talk proper'; but their membership of a state-culture was seldom seriously in doubt; nor was the identity of the state which was to provide the required protection. These people were seldom subjected to a tug of war between rival nationalists, claiming them to be 'really' members of A rather than B. In the main, they knew already what their identity was, and which state was charged with protecting that identity.

Zone 2

Immediately to the east of the coastal area, there is another region which deviates from the simplest path from nation-free to nationalist-prone society. This is the area corresponding roughly to the territory of the erstwhile Holy Roman Empire. Whereas, in the westernmost zone, the couple had been cohabiting for centuries before being called to do so by nationalism, here the situation was odd in a different kind of way: the bride had been ready, all tarted up at the altar, for a long long time, but, but ... no groom!

Unmetaphorically: a high, *staatsfähig* culture (the bride) had long been available among both Italians and Germans. In Italy since Dante and the early Renaissance, in Germany since Luther, or perhaps even since crusaders from different Teutonic language areas had to forge a standard speech when they were pushing East, a normative idiom endowed with writing and capable of providing the base for a national, culturally homogeneous state was to hand. The German literary revival at the end of the eighteenth century may have had to standardise orthograpy a bit, but basically a normative high culture was already there. Moreover, the peasant catchment area for these cultures was reasonably clear, continuous, identifiable and compact, except for the numerous pockets of Germans in eastern Europe – but this did not alter the fact that no cultural engineering, no culture-creation, was required.

But, and this was a big *but*: no state, no groom. Whereas strong dynastic states had crystallised on the Atlantic coast, and also in eastern Europe, this European zone was marked by political fragmentation. This is not the place to speculate why this should have been so: early commercial development strengthening independent cities, the conflict of Pope and Emperor, the terms of settlement at the end of the wars of religion – these may be candidates for the explanation. But, whatever the reason, come the Age of Nationalism, there *was* a well-developed national culture, but no state-protector. So, of course, Italian and German nationalism had to be concerned with *unification*.

In each case, a suitable groom was found: Piedmont and Prussia respectively. The groom was not necessarily over-enthusiastic – it was said that the Kaiser preferred to be King of Prussia. But the fact that it was primarily unification that was at stake, rather than 'liberation', that no cultural manipulation was required, and that the compactness of the territories to be unified dispensed with the need for ethnic cleansing – all this meant that at least nineteenth-century unificatory nationalism could be relatively benign and liberal, and could act in alliance with liberalism. No doubt it was also ruthless in its own way, and Cavour did make the comment that the means employed would make him a scoundrel, were they used in private life for personal ends. All the same, the amount of diplomatic chicanery and actual warfare required for the attainment of unification was not much larger, if larger at all, than that involved in the purely dynastic, ethnically irrelevant wars of the eighteenth century. (Why these nationalisms became virulent in the subsequent century is another question, to be discussed later.) Here was a kind of nationalism which only wished to confer a worthy political roof on a nation which already existed (or existed as much as those of the westernmost zone, where peasants also had to be taught to 'talk proper' and be informed of what their nation was and what it was called). The ethnographic map on the whole was not so complex as to make this aim attainable only through cleansing. A nation wanted its own state in addition to its own main poet, main opera and so on, and to satisfy this ambition, it was not obvious that it had to do down anyone else. A blessed condition, but not one necessarily repeated elsewhere, or destined to last.

Zone 3

It is when we move further east that the trouble really starts. In the second zone, nationalism *could* be benign and liberal; it had no inherent *need* to go nasty (even if in the end it did). In the third zone, on the other hand, violence and brutality seem to have been inscribed into the nature of the situation. The horror was not optional, it was predestined.

In eastern Europe, all in all, there were *neither* national states *nor* national cultures. In terms of our metaphor, neither groom nor bride was available. If the nationalist imperative – one state, one culture – was to be satisfied, and the passion for it in fact became very strong in the course of the nineteenth century, then both state and culture had to be created. Both political and cultural engineering were required. And the material on which the engineers were to work was such as to call for some rather brutal earth-shifting. It is the simultaneous creation of a national state and a national culture, in a social world lacking both, and endowed with an appallingly complex patchwork of linguistic and cultural differences, interspersed both on the map and in the social structure: it is this combination which is a recipe for catastrophe. The ingredients of this recipe were only too conspicuously present in eastern Europe.

It may be a slight exaggeration to say that eastern Europe had *no* national high cultures. The Poles, for instance, had one, and its glamour was sufficient that when a Lithuanian dynasty took over Poland, it was Polish culture which absorbed the Lithuanian gentry, and not the other way round. There are other nations which can make some kind of claim to cultural and/or political continuity. But the general point holds: there was a patchwork of cultures and languages, the folk languages were ill-defined and, for instance, in the case of Slavonic languages, it was exceedingly hard, or impossible, to say where one dialect ended and another one began, or what was a language and what was a dialect. For as liberal a man as Anton Chekhov, for instance, the Ukrainians were invisible: the *Cherry Orchard* is clearly intended to be a parable on *Russia*. But if you read the play with care, you find that it is all taking place in the Ukraine: the cherries are taken to be sold in Kharkov...

The states which did exist were only loosely connected with their own dominant ethnic group. In the Tsarist aristocracy, families of Tartar, Baltic or Georgian origin were prominent, no doubt over-represented in relation to the size of their ethnicity of origin, and certainly not discriminated against; and this is not to mention the position of outright foreigners in the military and civil service. The Russian commander in the Crimean war rejoiced in the splendid name of Todleben – a fine name for a soldier, but it is hardly Slavonic. In the Ottoman Empire, the Anatolian Turkish peasantry were exploited and oppressed, rather than being beneficiaries of their connection with the dominant *ethnie*. As for the cultures, in the main they had to be *created* in the nineteenth century, and the standardised, normative form had to be diffused, by methods which could be benign or brutal.

It was this situation, and the contrast between it and that which prevailed in the west of Europe, which led to the remarkable essay on nationalism by John Plamenatz (1973). John Plamenatz was a Montenegrin Wykehamist, not a terribly common combination. His father was a notable back in Montenegro and, it is said, one of the signatories of the peace at the end of the Balkan wars, and sufficiently well off to send his son to Winchester. Plamenatz was a very nice man who became Professor of Government in Oxford and, truth to tell, author of, on the whole, somewhat dull works on politics, with one outstanding exception, his remarkable essay on nationalism, which should have been called 'The sad reflections of a Montenegrin in Oxford'.

The main point of his essay, put simply, was that west of Trieste, nationalism could be benign, but east of Trieste it was likely to be horrible. This, on the surface, was a strange thing to say not very long after the demise of Hitler and Mussolini, who proved that nationalism west of Trieste could be as horrible as any. Nevertheless Plamenatz was making a profound point. The horror of Nazism and Fascism is optional. (Why it arose remains to be discussed.) The horror of nationalism to the east is inherent in the situation. Plamenatz could have predicted, though he did not formulate it in that way, the tragedy of the dissolution of Yugoslavia.

The basic point is simple: in conditions such as those which prevail in the Balkans, the Caucasus, the Volga bend, much of central Asia and many other parts of the world, culturally homogeneous nation-states, such as are held to be normative and prescribed by history in nationalist theory, can be produced only by ethnic cleansing. In such areas, either people must be persuaded to forgo the implementation of the nationalist ideal, or ethnic cleansing must take place. There is no third way.

Zone 4

Within eastern Europe, one can distinguish two zones: 3 and 4. The former has already been discussed. Zone 4 can be defined as the area which has passed through the period of Bolshevism. Just to complicate matters, this area expanded in 1945, with the westward advance of the Red Army and the imposition of Communist regimes in a large number of countries. Within zone 4, there are countries which were under Communism for roughly seventy years, and others for forty.

Zone 4 is, from the viewpoint of the development of nationalism, characterised by the fact that it passed more or less 'normally' through the first two stages, the Viennese and the Irredentist, but then something strange happened. At the end of the First World War, all three of the empires which had carved up eastern Europe between themselves in Vienna went on to the dustheap of history. But one of them was restored, fairly quickly, under a new management and under a new ideology. This new faith was upheld and implemented with great conviction, vigour and ruthlessness. The regime was incomparably more unscrupulous and murderous than the *anciens régimes* which had, all in all, held nationalism in check between 1815 and 1918. Not surprisingly, this system had no very great difficulty in suppressing and containing nationalism during the period of its existence. Contrary to some predictions and analyses, it was not nationalism which brought it down: it was defeat in the economic Cold War, the first major war to be fought by economic not violent means, and one which proved astonishingly conclusive in its outcome. Nationalism had not contributed much to this outcome, but benefited from it, and decisively contributed to the break-up of empire after economic defeat had, with astonishing candour, been conceded. Incidentally, the Soviet successor empire to the Tsars was also curiously non-national: as Russian nationalists complained and complain with some justice, Russians were not specially favoured in it. Some backwood parts of the Russian Republic were probably the most disadvantaged parts of the empire, and other nationalities – initially Jews, but later Georgians and Ukrainians – were prominent in the leadership of the Soviet Union.

The nature of the Communist regime and the causes of its demise are an enormous subject. From the viewpoint of following the differing trajectories of nationalism in various parts of Europe, this can be said: having passed through the first two stages, this part of Europe was spared the remaining three – for the time being. There were massive and brutal transfers of populations, but they did not, on the whole, simplify the ethnic map. (This does not apply to Poland and the Czech Republic.) They merely made it complex in a new way.

The crucial question is: now that the intervening force of Communism has disappeared, will the 'natural' development resume, and will it slot itself in at stage 3, 4 or 5? Shall we see the proliferation of small, weak, inexperienced and minority-haunted states, or ethnic cleansing, or a diminution of the intensity of the ethnic intrusion in politics? For much of ex-Yugoslavia, the answer is, alas, clear: it is ethnic cleansing, and indeed this is where the term was coined. Elsewhere, the answer is not yet clear. No doubt it will not be the same answer in all places. There is some evidence for each of the three options, and we do not yet know which one will predominate, and where.

EIGHT

The murderous virulence of nationalism

We have offered a 'normal' or 'natural' model of the stages of transition from non-nationalist traditional society to nationalism-prone modern society. We have refined or diversified it by specifying why this has played itself out to the full only in one of the four time zones of Europe. We have also indicated the additional factors which have modified the pattern in the other three zones. These factors were: the pre-existence of strong centralised states correlating, roughly, with cultural areas and so ready to become national states; the pre-existent availability of modern-type high cultures, only seeking a political partner so as to create a nation-state; and finally, the emergence and temporary domination, in one part of Europe, of a secular religion strong enough, for a time, to thwart nationalism.

This basic model, which offers an overall theory of nationalism, does not account for the extreme virulence of nationalism in Europe during the first half of our century, or worse still, it predicts virulence only for some parts of

Europe, but not for just those where in fact it was most extreme and murderous. The simple model offered, on its own, cannot explain this additional phenomenon. Can further factors, compatible with the model but not, at least visibly, corollaries of it, be invoked so as to make up this deficiency?

An argument will be offered in this chapter which endeavours to do precisely this. It does not have the simplicity of our overall model: this may be regretted by one who seeks elegance in theories, but it seems that it cannot be avoided. The world is a complex place, and, on occasion, factors do intrude which do not follow from simple premises, but have a kind of external or contingent quality. We can do no better than invoke these factors.

The additional factors, which are invoked to account for the extreme virulence of nationalism on certain occasions, are in part organisational and connected with the general forms of socioeconomic life at the time in question, and in part ideological. In part, perhaps, they are on the border of these two spheres.

Socioeconomic conditions

The economic distress caused by industrialism, both absolutely and relatively, is at its most acute during the early stages of economic development. The disruption of traditional rural life, the pauperisation of the erstwhile craftsmen, the arrival of a flood of indigent and disoriented newcomers in suddenly mushrooming early industrial cities, devoid of a material or an institutional or a moral infrastructure which would receive them – all this, in that West which enjoyed the *initium* of industrialisation, produced the world of Charles Dickens, and among the latecomers, the now familiar world of shantytowns, bidonvilles, *gecekondes*, where destitution may be absolutely worse than the 'idiocy of rural life' (Marx) which it replaces, and where the relative deprivation, in comparison with the beneficiaries of the first mounting wave of affluence, is hard to bear, given physical proximity and absence of the old legitimations of hierarchy. This is in itself explosive; but the explosion heralded by Marx and feared by Tocqueville (the evidence which inspired them was much the same) in the main only comes, as is now evident with the help of hindsight, if cultural ('ethnic') factors underscore the boundaries between incorporation and privilege, on the one side, and exclusion and poverty, on the other. Classes without ethnicity are blind; ethnicity without class is empty...

Cultural/organisational traditions

The factor which lies on the border between organisation and culture is this: the probability of violence is increased if the populations in question are drawn from areas in which relatively weak states permitted or encouraged a machismo ethic of self-help, where local communities were allowed to retain some of the prerogatives and obligations of the central order-maintaining agencies, and did so by inculcating in their members an ethos of honour, vengeance and the need for self-enforced legality. Societies in which men prove their manhood not by success in a career, but by quickness on the draw, may and do retain these values even when the unit on behalf of which offence is taken is no longer, or not exclusively, the local lineage, but the cultural category (i.e. 'the nation'). This condition seems to apply in large parts of the Balkans and no doubt helps explain the ferocity of ethnic conflict in this area, whether around 1912 or in the 1990s, or during the Second World War. There is a superb collection of short stories by Milovan Djilas, which are undeservedly less famous than some of his other work. They are obviously based on his personal experience of the guerrilla war against the Germans. The stories are full of killing, but note that they are almost never concerned with the killing of the German and Italian occupiers. The murdering is almost always *between* fellow South Slavs. No careful student of those stories would have been surprised by the tragedy following the dissolution of Yugoslavia.

Ideological factors

There is a further largely ideological factor which is also supremely important, and perhaps specially relevant to the twentieth-century virulence of nationalism in that zone which in the nineteenth century looked as if it might remain relatively benign (Germany and Italy). This element in the explanation is both important and complex, and deserves a chapter of its own.

NINE

The three stages of morality

For our purposes, humanity can be seen as having passed through three types of morality. First comes what may be called the morality of My Station and Its Duties. Plato was the supreme expositor of this vision: in *The Republic*, he defines justice (in effect, righteousness) as each part of the society performing its proper accredited task. (The same applies to the 'parts' of the soul. Sociopolitical strata and constituent parts of the psyche mirror each other, and both are ontologically vindicated: they inhere in the very nature of things.) For our purposes, this kind of ethic corresponds precisely to the *non*-national stage of human history: a man's identity and fulfilment are linked to his occupancy of a place in a stable and hierarchical social order. That order very probably (though not necessarily) involves cultural differences, sometimes great, sometimes subtle, between the various entrenched and sacralised strata; at the same time, no such cultural boundaries are needed to define the limits of political units, each of which is composed of parts which generally *are* distinguishable culturally. So, there is virtually no linkage between culture (i.e. ethnicity, nationality) and *either* the definition of the content of morality *or* the validating myth of morality, human fulfilment and respectworthiness.

So much for stage 1. Give or take points of detail, and occasional contingent fetishisation of culture, it applies to the entire agrarian world and stage of human history. Both the organisational principles and the accompanying ethos of this world were subjected to a scathing critique by the Enlightenment, a critique which could boast both brilliant literary expositors and very profound philosophical underpinning. The Enlightenment spurned the oppression, dogmatism, superstition and inequality sustained by phoney reasoning, which marked the *ancien régime. Ecrasez l'infâme!*

Its own ethic was individualistic, universalistic and egalitarian. The obligations and fulfilment of men flowed not from their status, but from their shared humanity. This generous morality had (at least) two variant formulations, one sensualistic, one rationalistic. Thinkers such as Hume found the basis of our morality in the fact that we were *sentient* human beings, capable of pleasure and pain, and capable of sympathy with the pain and pleasure of others. Thinkers such as Kant, on the other hand, located the source of our identity and morality in our shared *reason.* This distinction does not affect our argument: either way, the argument is cultureblind. What matters is that, whether our ultimate identity be sensitivity or reason, it is something universal and devoid of links with either cultural or political boundaries. It values neither of them, and can hardly be credited with preaching their apotheosis and the merit of their fusion. This kind of philosophy does not lend itself to nationalism, although, strangely and perversely, the late Elie Kedourie did single out Kant as a crucial progenitor of nationalism. What is true is that the individualistic, tradition-spurning philosophies of the Enlightenment, by helping to destroy the non-ethnic, communal or imperial polities of the pre-nationalist age, thereby also helped prepare the ground for nationalism.

But that in no way makes the severely individualist and universalist ethic of Kant, with its stress on *individual* self-determination, either the intellectual warrant or the historic cause of the doctrine of *national* self-determination. The words sound alike, but the meaning could hardly be more distant, or indeed more opposed. It is curious that, while Kedourie unjustly blames Kant, he just as unjustly exculpates Hegel, though he indisputably preached the fusion of state and nation: nations, in his view, only entered history proper when possessed of their own state...

Universalistic individualism is the second possible ethic, which succeeds, though of course never fully replaces, the morality of My Station and Its Duties. There follows a third kind of ethic, born of Romanticism and the reaction to the Enlightenment. It is supremely important for our argument and is considered in the next chapter.

TEN

Roots against reason

The first reaction against the rationalism of the Enlightenment came in literature. The coldness of the rationalist vision cast a pall over everything, and invaded areas, such as personal love, where it really seems offensive and to corrode that which we most value. Kant, as good an exemplar of the colder variety of Enlightenment vision as anyone, defined *love* as benevolence for duty's sake. Within the terms of his own philosophy, he had good reasons for so doing: *feelings* could not be commanded, they could not be part of our worth and our identity, and so love, in as far as it was commanded by the Christian morality (which he continued to uphold, claiming that it was simply a non-academic formulation of his own views), simply could not be the name of a sentiment. Sentiments were unworthy constituents of our human essence. What could be commanded, and what could be our true identity, was benevolence inspired by reverence for a universal law.

The poet Friedrich Schiller, himself a splendid specimen

of the Romantic reaction to the Enlightenment, ironised these views of Kant's, observing that his own benevolence to a friend was devalued by the fact that it was inspired and sustained by feeling. For Kant, something of the kind does indeed follow.

It might be supposed that the charge of arid rationalism, a commendation of a cold mentality untainted by feeling, could not be directed at a thinker such as David Hume, who is just as representative of the Enlightenment as Kant, but who makes *feeling* the very basis both of all conduct and of morality. Certainly, views such as Hume's must be considered: the Enlightenment reached its intellectual summit in Edinburgh as well as in Königsberg. But in fact, Hume exemplifies rather than contradicts our main point.

It is quite true, he does consider *feeling* to be the basis of morality, as indeed of all action. Only feelings can motivate, in his view, whether for moral or other conduct. But: what *kind* of feeling lies at the basis of morality? It is, says Hume, the feelings of an *impartial* observer, detached from his own position and vantage point. (The 'Veil of Ignorance' method of identifying justice, acclaimed as a recent academic discovery, has very old origins.) In this way, a universalism, a detachment from the local and specific, even if not free of all feeling, is also present in that version of Enlightenment doctrine which makes man the sentient being, rather than man the rational being, the foundation of everything.

And indeed, these are the two main and central points at which Romanticism opposes the Enlightenment: where the latter stressed reason and human universality, the former valued and praised feeling and specificity – above all, *cultural* specificity. The two negations were, of course, intimately linked to each other: where reason is universal in its prescriptions (what it deems valid is valid for *all* and *at all times* and *in all places*), emotions are linked to specific communities, to 'cultures', which are, precisely, associations engendered and sustained by shared sentiment, shared by the members, and *not* shared by outsiders, by non-members. The sentiments have no reasons, for if they did, the reasons if valid at all would be cogent for all, whether members or not. Rationality cannot, simply cannot, define the membership of exclusive clubs: feelings *can*. Nations, unlike the brotherhood of man favoured by the Enlightenment, are exclusive clubs. They are based on sentiment, partly because this alone is compatible with their *separateness*, and partly because this links them to the vitality, the colour of life, which is precisely the point at which the Romantics were most at odds with the Enlightenment. Its cold, bloodless rationalism and universalism separated it from life, warmth and feeling.

It was the literary Romantics who first turned against the Enlightenment, outraged by the intrusion of cold barren reason into spheres such as personal love and sexuality. But Romanticism was not due to remain restricted, either to literature or to fields such as personal life. In due course, it made itself as much at home in scholarship as in literature; and it extended the sphere of its influence from the personal to the political. It all happened, visibly and conspicuously, during the quarter-century of the revolutionary and Napoleonic wars: it had all started with a cult of *reason* (on one occasion actually incarnated by a naked actress in the course of a rationalist ritual), but it ended with a mystical Emperor-cult and indulgence in military adventure, undertaken in a virtually art-for-art's-sake spirit. During the period of *ennui* which followed the Restoration and the new peace, the Romantics could and did indulge in nostalgia for the excitement they had lost, and regretted the boredom they had gained.

As Romanticism expanded from literature into scholarship, one of the most significant figures was Herder. His basic message was that humanity was not composed of atomised individuals, whose essence was a universal reason and whose spatially and temporally specific traits were irrelevant, but, on the contrary, that it was composed of nations/cultures, and their essence and value lay precisely in their specificity. The value and merit of human beings lay not in what they all had in common, but in what distinguished various communities from each other. It was this diversity and cultural specificity which really mattered.

Romanticism was almost ideally suited to provide nationalism with its idiom and its style. And so it did. Had commercialism and/or industrialism led, as liberalism and Marxism expected, to an irresistible all-embracing melting-pot and a universal humanity, then indeed the original philosophy of the Enlightenment would have provided it with a perfect ideological cover. But, for whatever reasons (and we have considered them), this did not happen: at least so far, the push towards homogeneity, towards *Gleichschaltung*, is engendering not one universal culture, but a finite number of internally standardised but externally differentiated 'national' cultures. These cultures define and *make* nations: it is not the case, as nationalists believe and proclaim, that independently and previously existing nations seek the affirmation and independent life of 'their' culture. Cultures 'have' and make nations; nations initially neither exist nor have or do anything. High cultures and homogeneity replace low cultures and diversity, and become politically significant: so-called 'nations' are simply the political shadows of this basic fact.

The early Herderian cult of communal differentiation and specificity was relatively modest, almost humble, rather than vicious and lethal. It merely praised and valued diversity, and it opposed the reduction of all mankind to a single model, to Versailles or Manchester: it resisted both the cultural imperialism of the French, which had so effectively conquered the courts and aristocracies of most of Europe, and British commercialism and empiricism. (Oswald Spengler maintained that what the French armies did during their Napoleonic domination of continental Europe was to spread *British* ideas. One suspects that the Imperial Guard was quite unaware of the fact that it was the agent of Adam Smith and David Hume.) Herder's modest commendation of folk culture and diversity clearly had its attractive side.

But as the nineteenth century progressed, the articulation of Romanticism in scholarship and science acquired a new potent ally, from biology: Darwinism. The doctrine that man is merely one further animal, and that he owes his propensity for violent competition to Natural Selection, has powerful political and philosophical implications. If he is just one further animal, what justification remains for giving himself airs and claiming to be discontinuous with nature? What justification remains for claiming a unique characteristic called reason? (The Enlightenment or some of its members had already been tempted by such a view, but lacked biological support for it.) Was it not plausible to suspect that so-called reason was but the pursuit of instinctual satisfactions by other means? If ruthless competition has brought us where we are, might it not be a permanent precondition of excellence, psychic health and genuine fulfilment? Nietzsche articulated ideas of this kind, blending the literary Romantic tradition with the real or alleged lessons drawn from biology.

The fusion of Herderian communalism and cult of specificity, with Darwinism as mediated by the romantic Nietzsche, was really explosive. The community was to be not merely culturally, but also biologically distinctive: it was not merely to defend and protect its own cultural specificity; it was to affirm it politically with an aggressiveness which was more of an end than a means, which was the expression and precondition of true vitality. By contrast, the bloodless universalism of the Enlightenment was an expression of the low cunning of the weak, the secular reformation of the old whining religion of the feeble; it was pathogenic and the expression of pathology.

This message – a plausible continuation of several deep strains of European thought and feeling (notably, of the naturalism of the Enlightenment and the Romantic cult of aggression and turbulence) – coincided with the maximum point of economic distress produced by industrialism/capitalism. There was a groundswell against this distress and against the universalist ideology claiming to validate it, a reaction which turned towards the old agrarian martial values, and which retained the agrarian equation of wealth with land (*Lebensraum*). In such a context the appeal of nationalism was powerful indeed. The first half of the twentieth century witnessed the simultaneous presence of all these factors and, indeed, their political expression. This is the best explanation we can offer of the quite remarkable virulence of nationalism in that period.

ELEVEN

Roots and man

Traditional society had taught that man was made by his status. The Enlightenment (perhaps secularising the religious view that man was made by his relation to a single deity) taught that man was made by his reason. Romanticism taught that he was made by his roots.

The dominance of the idea of 'roots' was underwritten by Romanticism, and fully satisfied the requirements of nationalism. It reflected the prevalence of culturally homogeneous, internally undifferentiated, cultural polities, known as 'nation-states'. A political unit was to be defined as the voluntary, indeed the emotionally compulsive, association of men of the same 'roots'. This freed the polity from being a system of statuses and, by allowing a 'return to the roots', did not insist that the identity of culture be there from the start: it was enough if there was a recollection of origins and a deep desire to return to the sources of one's vitality and true identity. It mattered little that the recollection might be a little suspect, that what was remembered was not too scrupulously checked for historical accuracy.

Nationalism, in as far as it liked to see itself as a repudiation of bloodless cosmopolitanism and as a return to the past and its values, and in as far as it (quite mistakenly) liked to attribute an ancient lineage to itself, tended to overrate the extent to which the past had indeed been concerned with ethnicity and culture in politics, and to be a bit selective in its recognition of the role of hierarchy in the past. It might, in its virulent form, make a cult of discipline, faith and subordination, but it had to ignore or play down the extent to which those warriors of old were touchy about status and indifferent to cultural similarity.

This notion of *roots* rather than status or reason as the basis of identity had a powerful appeal and profound implications. These deserve to be spelt out.

If roots are what make you what you are, endow you with both vigour and authenticity, it follows that rootlessness is the greatest of all sins, and terms such as *déraciné* and *cosmopolitan* carry the greatest opprobrium. Superficial smart alecks with a shallow urban cleverness, who can assume any accent and are committed to none, are the very model of a moral pathology. They above all are to be spurned, avoided and excluded. The universalist humanism of the Enlightenment had, of course, been the expression of their interests and attitude: it had suited them only too well! We are no longer to be deceived. Once upon a time, these over-urbanised, calculating, rootless operators had been defined in terms of formal religious faith. In the old days of the rigid, status-ascriptive social order, it was not easy to change one's faith, and this method served well enough to insulate them in their ghettos. Now, however, we live in a liberal world which permits men to change their religious denominations with ease, and so nominal religion will no longer serve for segregating the rootless from those endowed with blessed and genuine roots. So, if they are to be excluded, and excluded they must be, we must switch from asking people about their faith to asking them about their grandparents.

This was, of course, precisely what happened. The reorganisation of society, from rigid hierarchical structures to mobile pools of men sharing the same high culture and protected by the same political authority, led to a great preoccupation with *roots*. This mystique of rural roots (*soil*) was functional in helping to exclude urban specialised strata, too advantageously placed given the new rules of the game (meritocracy, semantic work, high valuation of mental agility). At the same time, it fitted in perfectly with the Romantic philosophy which provided the new nationalism with its rationale and its idiom.

It must be repeated that nationalism is a phenomenon of *Gesellschaft* using the idiom of *Gemeinschaft*: a mobile anonymous society simulating a closed cosy community. It is engendered, basically, by two facts: the dissolution of the old rigid hierarchical order in which most men knew their place and were glued to it, and the fact that the new order, because of the nature of work within it, needs to operate in a high culture. These high cultures then serve as boundary markers for both cultural ('national') and political boundaries, the two being required to be as congruent as possible.

A society run in the nationalist idiom in some ways resembles both the old static order and a fully mobile, universalistic society. It resembles the latter in its internal mobility and homogeneity, and the fact that its culture is one educationally transmitted, rather than 'learned on the job'. But the mobility is not unrestricted: it has its limits, and the terminology which allows those limits to be set, and which is itself linked to a plausible background myth, is that of 'roots'. The shift from history to biology as the main mythopoeic science helps this along, as does vitalism: vigour and health are linked to soil, to peasantry and, ironically, to that outdoor manual labour, the virtual disappearance of which from the real base of social life contributed so much to the original rise of nationalism. Romanticism, communalism, populism, vitalism and biologism all combine to endow the policy of citizenship-through-roots, and the persecution of the rootless, with a rationale well connected to many of the themes which in any case pervade European thought.

≡TWELVE

Faith and culture

We have focused on the transformation of society by industrialism as the main progenitor of nationalism. A mobile
society sharing a high (codified, literate) culture, and using
it as its main tool of work, defines and delimits its members
not by status but by culture, or by eligibility-into-a-culture
(known as 'roots'). This membership, or set of qualifications
for membership, becomes a person's most valuable possession, for it is virtually the precondition of the enjoyment
of or access to all other goods. Hence his main political
preoccupation must be to ensure the congruence of his own
(high) culture with that of the surrounding bureaucracies
(which, in the modern world, are almost certain to all employ
the *same* idiom: gone are the days when clerics spoke one
tongue, soldiers another, merchants another still, and so on).
Hence, if there is a discrepancy between the two, between
his own language and that of his social milieu, he will become
either an assimilationist or a nationalist, or indeed both at
once.

But while it is indeed industrialism which is the main force conducive to this condition, there are also other social features, which may accompany it or may have arrived independently, which also contribute to a similar end. Two of them are of particular importance: bureaucratisation and 'Protestant-type' religion. The bureaucratisation of an empire means that local administrators are appointed from the centre and sent out to their posts (instead of the centre selecting a person with a pre-existing local power-base as its agent). Bureaucrats receive similar training, implement similar rules and communicate with each other and with the centre in accordance with prescribed norms and in a shared idiom. If the bureaucracy lasts and is effective, its idiom is liable to become the language of the entire society, either right down into the intimacy of family life, or at least at the level of public business. Something like this seems to have happened among the Han Chinese, to Latin in the Western Roman Empire, and to Greek in the Eastern and Byzantine empires.

It is the other factor, 'Protestant-type' religion, which concerns us here. A religion is Protestant in type if it eliminates or radically diminishes mediation between the laity and the transcendent, and in effect turns all members of the religious community into priests: it effects the universalisation of priesthood, every man being his own priest. Second, it tends to focus on faith, doctrine and scripture, to the detriment of ritual and 'works'. In order to believe in his faith, the believer has to know what it is; as he is his own priest, he has to have access to it; and as it happens to be available in the holy writ, he has to be able to read. This cogent chain of reasoning makes Protestantism a powerful agent of the diffusion of literacy. Protestantism, by translating scripture into the vernacular, is normally credited with rendering salvation more directly accessible, which indeed it does. But at the same time, it not only spreads Truth downwards, it elevates the vernacular into a high culture. If the faithful are to read about the path to salvation in their own dialect, that dialect must be given its alphabet and codified sufficiently to make publication in it feasible.

Thus Protestantism achieves, for its own religious ends, that transformation of a peasant dialect into a 'real' language, codified and capable of transmitting messages in a context-free manner over distances and over a large anonymous population. That which, later, nationalism strove to do, and did, for overtly political ends, Protestantism practised earlier, and, at least initially, in a politically innocent manner.

Protestantism advances the social position of a vernacular, turning it into the medium of a high culture, in order to advance a *faith*. In so doing, it helps prepare the ground for the emergence of a nation, which may or may not remain linked to that faith, loyal to it, and defined in part in terms of adherence to it. Nationalism, by contrast, pushes a vernacular in the direction of a high culture, and may avail itself of the help of the faith, which may have already done a good deal to further literary codification, and whose personnel may be eager to help in the process of mixed religious and national missionary work. The two processes are lined, but they are also distinct and separable. Bernard Shaw expressed the thought when he caused his St Joan to be burnt as a Protestant by the Church and as a nationalist by the English. On his account, she was both (though at the same time, she had little sympathy for the Bohemian Hussites, whose historic role is even more clearly tinged with the ambiguity between Protestantism and nationalism).

The two processes, nationalism and Protestantism, clearly do have an affinity both in their guiding ideas and in their social consequences. Nevertheless, the important fact in European history is that, on the whole, the two trends have separated: on balance, the Age of Nationalism in Europe is also an Age of Secularism. Nationalists love their culture because they love their culture, not because it is the idiom of their faith. They may value their faith because it is, allegedly, the expression of their national culture or character, or they may be grateful to the Church for having kept the national language alive when otherwise it disappeared from public life; but in the end, they value religion as an aid to community, and not so much in itself.

This generalisation, which all in all is valid in Europe, no doubt requires qualification. French chauvinism, for instance, was often also virulently Catholic; Polish nationalism and Catholicism would be hard to separate; certain nations, such as Serbs, Croats and Bosnians, are very nearly definable only by their religion (or the religion they lost), being linguistically and 'racially' more or less indistinguishable from precisely those 'nations' with which they are locked in conflict. However, these qualifications, important though they are, do not in the end overturn the generalisation. A Pole may by definition be a Catholic (there are a few Protestants, once they were more numerous, and the Protestants are not unpatriotic), and the Church may have provided an invaluable counter-state in the days of struggle with Communism; but it is questionable whether we are dealing with a belief, as opposed to a symbol of identity (Mach 1985). The Poles may have used the faith and its organisational expression to great effect in the struggle with the Communist regime, which enabled them to make an outstanding contribution to its termination; but it is more a case of a secular nationalism using a faith than the other way round.

This would seem to be the European pattern. Need it always be so? The development of Islam in the twentieth century suggests that there is another possibility.

⹀THIRTEEN

Muslim fundamentalism and Arab nationalism

The question put at the end of the previous chapter – how can the elaboration and social diffusion of a vernacular-derived high culture be separated from the faith which frequently inspired the codification of that culture? – enables us to add a further, fifth, zone to our earlier geographical typology. We had the European zone where culture had married the state by accident even before the age of nationalism; the zone where culture was providentially ready but needed to find her protector; the zone where all five stages of a painful transition had to be traversed before a nation-state was available; and the zone in which the development was distorted by the superimposition of the Bolshevik ideocracy. Leaving in the main, the limits of Europe, we reach a fifth zone: that of Islam. Thereby we also reach an area in which the question concerning the linkage and severance of faith and culture received an answer radically different from the one visible in Europe: we may hope that this difference will help illuminate the general relationship between culture and faith.

In the nineteenth and twentieth centuries (but largely in the twentieth), the world of Islam had undergone a transformation similar to that which had begun sooner in Europe, and which we invoke in our explanation of political nationalism. The overwhelming majority of the population lived locked into local communities: social position was imposed on most men by birth. There was a considerable stability of social and economic structure: when there was turbulence and violence, the social order was much the same at the end of it as it had been at the beginning, even if there was a turnover of personnel.

The religious expression of this situation was fairly clear. The local group which played so important a part in social life were serviced by a proliferation of 'saints' and saint cults and organisations which appear in the western literature as religious orders or brotherhoods. The two things are not really distinct, in as far as these orders or fraternities are defined by their devotion to a founding saint. The absence of any requirement or expectation of celibacy permits descendants of founding saints to serve as a kind of surrogate clergy (formally, Islam has none), and to be 'saints' themselves. It is reasonable to describe this situation in terms of the sociology of religion formulated by Emile Durkheim: the religious was the expression of the social. The saints helped the social units to articulate themselves. One might add that, very typically, the saints defined not a lay group, but the boundary between groups. Most of these saints were credited with an ancestry which made them into the descendants of the Prophet. This also served a purpose: the saints constituted a link between folk piety, full of what a purist might consider alien elements, and the official faith in the keeping of the scholars.

That, roughly speaking, was the old order. Apart from the popular Islam of the saints, there was also an Islam of scholars, endowed with more 'Protestant' traits, such as a stress on unitarianism, condemnation of mediation (technically, this constitutes the sin of *sirk*), scripturalism and puritanism. It is open to dispute how far the two styles of faith were in conflict or in harmony (cf. Zubaida 1995). Arguments and evidence can be invoked on both sides: unquestionably, the two styles often lived in peaceful co-existence, with urban scholars also being members of saint-based orders, and rustic saints implicitly recognising, through the themes of their legends, the normative authority of more scholarly urban religion. Such a mutual interpenetration unquestionably existed. However, on the other side, one can invoke the emergence of anti-saint movements such as the Wahabis of central Arabia, a movement which began in the eighteenth century, well before the impact of western modernity in the region.

This issue will no doubt continue to be the object of learned and illuminating debate; it certainly is not settled. What, however, is not in question is that, by about the beginning of the twentieth century, a movement was under way which firmly commended reform, and which is itself committed to a 'purer', i.e. less popular, less mediationist, more scripturalist and puritanical Islam. The question the reformers faced was: why did we fall behind the West? Why was Islam, once so confident and dominant, subjected to the humiliation of alien and infidel conquest and influence? The answer offered had some small elements of 'westernisation', but in the main, the recommendation was a return to the origin, to the sources, to purity, to, if you like, *roots*.

So far, one might discern a measure of similarity with eastern Europe: its élites, finding their societies backward in comparison with the West, were torn between a 'westernising' and a populist tendency. Russian literature of the nineteenth century is, of course, the classical and superb expression of this tension. The populists looked towards 'the people', but they also looked towards the old faith, and tended to conflate the two. The Slavophils were in a way, Orthodoxy-phils. All Slavs are Slavs, but Orthodox ones are more so: an element of this attitude survived right into the 1990s, and an element of it could on occasion be discerned in the Russian attitude to the Yugoslav conflict – though it should be added that in the new Russian right, there is also a deviant segment which finds the Russian soul not in

Orthodoxy but in Slav paganism. Far from Prince Vladimir having converted to Christ in response to popular demand, in fact it was just a political ploy and the real *narod* remained true, for a long time, to the old gods. Orthodoxy was just the first of the Zionist-Masonic plots...

However, there is a profound and important difference between east European and Muslim reactions to backwardness or 'underdevelopment'. When the Russian populists turned to the people, they were primarily concerned with the people as such, and the faith was incorporated *because* it was the faith of simple people. It was vindicated by the alleged virtues of those who held it, rather than the other way round. In the world of Islam, it *was* the other way around. *Roots* had a theological, Revelation-linked rather than populist meaning. There is little or no populism in Islam. Muslims leave the idealisation of simple people to outsiders, so that it tends to be practised vicariously, by the likes of T. E. Lawrence or General Daumas or Alois Musil.

When the Muslim reformers commended a return to roots, they meant not to the simple people, but to the original Revelation as transmitted to the Prophet, and as practised by Him and His Companions. How accurate their historical image of the first generations of Islam is does not concern us. Concretely, the image they had of the purity of the original faith corresponded to a more puritan, scripturalist, unitarian, mediation-free, sober Islam of the High Tradition, as practised by themselves. It was not the people who were the 'roots': on the contrary, the sad truth was that the *people*, the untutored rural and urban masses, represented corruption and ignorance, a sliding away from the true faith and its practices, a regression which was blamed for the decline of Muslim fortunes and the humiliating condition of early twentieth-century Islam.

East Europeans, when facing the problem of the backwardness of their own societies, in the end faced the dilemma between idealising the West, or idealising the virtues of their own 'people'. Not so in Islam: the dilemma became emulating the West (liberalism, technicism, nationalism, Marxism, etc.), or setting up as a rival model a genuinely present local tradition, which however was a tradition incarnated by an urban scholarly élite, not by folk culture. This was the basic stance and message of the reform movement, and the difference with the European situation is profound.

And so is, at any rate so far, the end result. For a long time, nationalism and even various forms of Marxist-nationalist syncretism were prominent. Islamism and nationalism could also co-exist: it was not clear whether Islam deserved praise for being the social cement of the Arabs, or whether Arabs deserved respect for being the carriers of Islam. Ambiguities of this kind are not uncommon in the ideological life of societies. But by now, much of the ambiguity is dispersed: fundamentalism has emerged as the dominant and victorious trend. Whether this will continue to be so we do not know: prophecy is dangerous, and it is not being attempted here. But the situation at present seems clear.

The transition from closed, stable and culturally diversified communities to standardised, mobile, anonymous mass societies is taking place among Muslims, as it has in the West. But in the West, the cultural standardisation and the pre-eminence of high culture expressed itself above all as nationalism, in which the new high culture is revered *as such*, in its own name: the faith and its organisation receive implicitly condescending praise for having sustained, aided and expressed the culture or, as it is now conceived, the 'national spirit'. It is not valued on its own terms, as the expression of an authoritative, transcendent, extraneous Revelation: such claims, it is quietly (and sometimes overtly) implied, are just a manner of speaking. It is ourselves, our way of life, that we revere and worship, and if we use a transcendent or Biblical idiom for so doing, well, you understand, one has to use *some* language. It was the only one to hand at the time ...

Not so in Islam. The generalised new high culture is prevailing not in the name of its folk roots, but in the name of its links to a faith which is taken with utmost seriousness, indeed literally with lethal seriousness. The roots which matter are in the transcendent and not in the soil. The Uncreated Word of God, not peasant wisdom, vindicates the new culture.

It is not clear why the victory of a standardised high culture in mobile anonymous societies, which live increasingly by semantic not physical work, should take the form of nationalism in Europe and of fundamentalism in Islam. We have indicated some of the differential factors in the background which may contribute to an explanation, but it would be idle to pretend that a fully convincing explanation is ready to hand. Islam is unique among world religions, in being, so far, clearly incompatible with the widely held secularisation thesis, which maintains that the social and psychic hold of religion diminishes with industrialism. The extent to which this is true in other civilisations is open to debate; that it is true to some extent is not. In Islam, it is not true at all. An explanation of this fact will presumably overlap with the explanation of the victory of fundamentalism over nationalism.

⹏FOURTEEN

Marxism and Islam

The twentieth century has witnessed two major surprises in the field of ideology: the strong, vigorous, secularisation-resistant character of Islam, and the sudden, total, unopposed and ignominious collapse of Marxism. Neither of these was anticipated or predicted by social scientists. All in all, they expected the secularisation thesis, which affirms that religion declines in power in an industrial age, to apply to Islam as much as to other religions; and as for Marxism, it was generally regarded as a secular religion, which was endowed with all the strengths and weakness of religions proper. That it would become routinised, that its ardour would diminish, all that was to be expected; but it was assumed that those who lost their enthusiasm would nevertheless retain their piety, and that there would be a reasonable proportion of zealots who would remain committed to the faith in all its purity and force.

Something of this kind constituted the conventional wisdom on the matter, and it all seemed plausible enough.

But time has given it disproof. In as far as both these creeds have their involvements, their affinities and oppositions with nationalism, it is appropriate to ask what explanations can be offered for the unexpected and highly contrasted differences in their actual fates. In fact, Marxism had on occasion been characterised as the Islam of our age: it had the simplicity, the messianism, the moralism, the prediction and obligation of a Holy War which in the end was bound to be victorious. So what went wrong?

The respective relationships of Islam and Marxism to nationalism differ. Neither really has room for it. Islam has its *Umma*, the charismatic community of the faithful, but that is not an ethnic group, even if it has a deep affinity for one culture, in as far as God speaks Arabic. Marxism knows classes not nations: only classes are legitimate communities and in the end only one class is legitimate. Marxism legitimates, not so much the state, but the blessed transformation which renders the state redundant. In practice, Islam in the twentieth century overcame nationalism without even deliberately combating it and while, on our argument, performing most of the functions normally served by nationalism. Marxism, by contrast, consciously fought nationalism and defeated it, at any rate in areas where it had the advantage of controlling the state, though not in areas where it had to compete in an open ideological market. On the other hand, when the state or state-system it had erected in its heyday collapsed, Marxism was swept away with it like the snows of yesteryear, and provided nationalism with no serious competition at all. If anything, in a watered-down, ideologically unspecific and undemanding form, it actually often combined with it, in that rather repugnant red-brown alliance which is conspicuous in the politics of a number of ex-Communist countries.

Why this marked and extreme difference in the destiny of two faiths, which had previously been considered similar, deep down, by many observers? We can only propound hypotheses in answer to this question: the answer is not yet within our grasp, if it ever will be.

Islam is in many ways astonishingly modern. It preaches a severe monotheism, with a low load of magic and a heavy weight of morality; it proscribes mediation, thereby insisting on a direct relationship between believer and deity, and a symmetrical situation for all the faithful. For Hegel, as the philosopher who saw history as the gradual and progressive revelation of a divine plan, the fact that Islam was subsequent to Christianity was an embarrassment (if Christianity was the highest and final religion, it should also have been the last); he had to surmount this little difficulty with some rather devious reasoning. In fact, Hegel's full problem should have been not merely chronological, but also qualitative: by many of the criteria accepted as valid by the modern world, Islam is not merely *later*, but also qualitatively superior. Max Weber has on the whole replaced Hegel (and his disciple Marx) as the main theoretician of the emergence of modernity, but Islam is just as much a problem for him: if modern, dis-interested productive and organisational rationality was an unintended by-product of the anxiety of the earnest believer facing a moralistic *and* predestinarian God, why on earth did that rationality not burst upon the world among the Muslim urban bourgeoisie? Why are those urban Muslims, when not humiliated by the outside world, so dreadfully at peace with themselves, so free of that inner tormenting anxiety which was to possess their European equivalents and drive them to accumulate for the sake of accumulation?

The fact that the modern world did not emerge from the womb of Islam can perhaps be explained in terms of the overall political structure of Muslim states (Turner 1974): the urban bourgeoisie was too frightened of the tribal country-side to secure independence or a share of government for itself. It preferred the Sultan's extortions to tribal pillage. The curious thing is, however, that when the modern world did come, initiated elsewhere and imposed from outside, this bourgeoisie still did not perform quite as well in the economic stakes as might have been expected, if the Web-erian thesis about the link between puritan anxiety and econ-omic effectiveness were valid.

If Islam neither initiated modernity, nor turned out to do exceptionally well when it arrived, it has shone, as we insist, in a different and important way: its vigour in the modern world remains undiminished or is enhanced. Is there an explanation?

Tentatively, we can offer this one: though modern (unitarian, low load of magic, symmetry of believers with each other, a distant deity), it is not *too* modern. It does not deify the world: the object of reverence remains extraneous, transcendent. Life in the world is highly regulated, but it retains its mundane, profane status. The sacred and the profane remain distinct, as Durkheim insisted they must be, and they do not sully each other. It is not merely that the divine is a refuge from the earthly, but the earthly is also a refuge from the excessive demands and exaltation of the religious. Islam dominates and regulates but does not sacralise daily life and, in particular, economic life.

By contrast, just this was perhaps the crucial philosophic mistake of Marxism. Its central philosophic intuition was the abolition of the bifurcation of existence into this world and the other. It not merely proscribed the use of the other world for consolation and escape, but also, fatally, prescribed reverence for *this* world and our activity in it. Not for nothing was it intellectually descended, through Hegel, from Spinoza's pantheism, his sense of the unity and sacredness of this world. What brought Bolshevism down in the end was perhaps not its lack of the sacred but, on the contrary, its lack of the profane. When the economic and normally profane realm became, in the age of stagnation, unquestionably squalid, it could not be downgraded and routinised: it was, after all, the very home of the sacred; work was the essence of man, and the sacrament of the new order. When the sacrament turns out to be as squalid as indeed it was under Brezhnev, faith must go, and faith did go. It had survived (indeed flourished) under the massive and random bloodletting under Stalin, but it could not survive this.

So perhaps the lesson of the two most unexpected events of the twentieth century is this: a high level of modernity (symmetry, morality not magic, non-mediation, trans-cendence of the sacred) helps a faith to survive in the modern world. But total modernity (abolition of the sacred/profane distinction, sacralisation of this world) does not seem well adapted to the real requirements of our situation. Marxism can suppress, though not eliminate, nationalism when it is in control of the state and can use its sanctions; otherwise, it cannot compete with it. Islam appears capable of competing successfully with nationalism, whether or not it is in control of the state.

FIFTEEN

Do nations have navels?

Perhaps the major debate which has arisen in the theory of nationalism of late occurs between primordialists and modernists. The issue is simple: is the sense of ethnicity, the identification with a 'nation', and the political expression of this passionate identification, something old and present throughout history, or is it, on the contrary, something modern and a corollary of the distinctive feature of our recent world? The present book is, of course, firmly on the latter side, but this does not prevent it, one hopes, from presenting the issues in a clear and unprejudicial manner.

As so often, not one, but several overlapping questions are involved. At the most abstract level, one is dealing with the metaphysical question of the reality of the past and the present. It was Bertrand Russell, I think, who once played with the following conundrum: how do we know the world was not created five minutes ago, complete with memories and, naturally, the whole complement of historical, arch-eological and geological records? What conceivable difference would there be, *now*, between such a world, and the world which in fact we think we inhabit: that is, a world which has been here for quite some time? The question poses a problem for any radical empiricist, who would maintain that two propositions only have distinct meanings if evidence is conceivable which would support the one, but contradict the other. *Ex hypothesi*, there is no piece of evidence, at any rate in the present or the future, which could distinguish between the hypothesis of a world created complete with memories and records, and the hypothesis of a long-established world, which had 'genuinely' accumulated the record and the memories. As we only have access to evidence in the present or the future, it follows that we cannot possess evidence on the basis of which we could rationally choose between the two hypotheses, which are consequently identical by extreme empiricist criteria, but profoundly different intuitively and to common sense.

There is a certain similarity between this question and the extreme version of the opposition between Evolutionists and 'Creationists', as the confrontation developed under the impact of Darwinism. One suggestion made was that the issue could be decided by finding out whether or not Adam had a navel: if, as the Biblical account affirms, he was directly created by God, clearly there was no reason why he should have a navel. However, not all Creationists accepted this argument: if God created the world at a given moment, things could only function if they had the structure *they would have had*, had they existed for some time. For instance, rivers would already be flowing, as opposed to having to wait to be filled by wholly new springs. So God would create riverbeds already filled, as if they had been flowing for ages, and similarly, Adam would be endowed with a perfectly pointless navel. This argument can then be, quite logically, extended: God would also create geological strata, fossils, etc. *as if* the world had existed for a long time, and so permit geologists and others to reconstruct a non-existent, but internally coherent past.

On this issue, which divides fundamentalist believers from

Darwinists, it is the adherents of traditional common sense who uphold Creation, and the upholders of the authority of Science who defend the evolutionist view. In the debate concerning nationalism, it is the other way round: common-sense popular belief is on the side of the antiquity of nation and nationalist sentiment, whereas it is we rather modernist thinkers, eager to practise science in the social sphere, who are Creationists. We believe in the Creation of Nations, not in a week, but in a couple of centuries or so. The alignments are inversed, but the logic of the debate is similar. Hence my question: do nations have navels?

There is an artificiality about the very general formulation of the question ('can the past *ever* be real?') which inclines one to dismiss it as 'metaphysical' in a pejorative sense, implying that the issue is simultaneously difficult and trivial. Yet there is an element of just this issue in the debate between primordialists and modernists. The modernist is, at least in part, motivated by this very general consideration: after all, only the present can be operative in the present. The past is dead, gone, unreal: no past force can act *now*, because it is, indeed, *past*; it has 'passed'. It is not present here and now, so it cannot make any difference here and now.

This argument is quite often present in the human and social sciences and is liable to influence research and explanatory strategies: for instance, in economics, anthropology or psychonalysis. In economics, it takes the form of stressing the relevance of *present* supply and demand (never mind 'historic' costs). In anthropology it is known as 'functionalism' and the recommendation to explain societies in terms of the synchronic interaction of institutions rather than in terms of the past. In psychoanalysis the same argument emerges as the stress on the actual therapeutic situation and interaction, as opposed to the alleged influence of distant traumata.

This very general consideration is involved, but clearly it is not the whole story. A 'modernist' theorist of nationalism, such as myself, considers *nationalism* to be an inherently modern phenomenon, but he does not consider all social phenomena to be modern, or everything to be made over new in the modern age. On the contrary, he believes both culture and power to be perennial, but to be related to each other in a new way in the modern age, a way which then engenders nationalism. So what else is involved?

It is a question of continuity or, rather, a whole set of related continui*ties*: do cultures, power structures, the recognition of a given culture as a thing, an entity (as an object of love, loyalty and identification), and the *political* use of cultural identification and differentiation – do all these persist across the boundary, wherever exactly it is to be drawn, between the traditional and the modern? A primordialist is a man who repudiates the suggestion that 'nations', and the idea that they are at the root of political obligation, have been invented (eve if not consciously) in modern times. The primordialist refuses to accept that the attribution of an immemorial antiquity to nations is a illusion. Whether or not the primordialist is himself a nationalist, whether he reveres some particular culture/nation and believes it to be hallowed by age, at any rate he sympathises with the nationalist who insists on the genuine antiquity (never mind the periods of somnolence induced by enemies) of his nation. By contrast, the modernist considers this antiquity to be either an illusion or an irrelevance.

What evidence could decide this issue? Here we are no longer in the realm of two hypotheses, intuitively incompatible with each other, but, both of them, equally compatible with all available evidence.

As stated, what is at issue is *continuity*. Are cultures continuous and, often, continuous right across historical watersheds between one form of social organisation and another? The answer is, unquestionably, *yes*. Culture *is* something transmitted over time. Yet the very diversity of cultures which is of the essence of humanity also includes diversity over time: cultures can change fast, and sometimes do so. It is precisely the shift from genetic to cultural transmission which makes possible, on a shared genetic base, the astonishing diversity of cultures and the possibility of very rapid change. So there is no general answer: cultures persist and cultures change. The striking empirical evidence points *both* ways. On the one hand, the historians and social scientists who have focused on the *Invention of Tradition* (Hobsbawm and Ranger 1983) have cogently demonstrated that what passes for ('continuous', 'immemorial') tradition is frequently invented (sometimes consciously) and of recent date, and that its validating antiquity is often spurious. At the same time, the experience of 'modernisers' who attempt to reorganise the structure of a given society is often that, notwithstanding organisational changes, a certain style of doing things may have an astonishing tenacity, and survive radical reorganisation. So, both these points are valid. Cultures are both tenacious and volatile. It is neither true that they are virtually immutable, like some slow-moving glacier which only shifts a few metres every year, preserving continuity while changing, nor is it the case that they are ever reinvented, ever spurious in their pretence of continuity. *Both* things happen, and if there are any laws concerning which predominates, we do not know them.

Cultures are sometimes invisible to their bearers, who look through them like the air they breathe, and sometimes heavily underscored and objects of great reverence and passion. There is, it seems to me, no valid general rule affirming either the volatility or the fidelity of men *vis-à-vis* their cultures. This is something which needs to be explored, by concrete historical and ethnographic research: abstract argument can and does provide us with plausible, sometimes persuasive models, but it cannot on its own clinch the matter.

In anthropology and the social sciences more generally, there has of late been a certain vogue for exclusive preoccupation with 'culture', its diversity and ultimacy. This vogue has various roots, which it would not be appropriate to explore here. What is relevant here is to stress the damage this vogue does to the advancement of understanding in the field which concerns us: by seeking primarily or exclusively 'cultural' rather than organisational explanations, this trend prejudges, unjustifiably, a most important question concerning the relative importance of structural and cultural factors. (It is quite possible that there is no *general* answer to this question, that the relative importance of the two types of cause varies from case to case and situation to situation.) The exclusive culturalism or hermeneuticism or interpretivism, to mention some of the available appellations for this trend, makes it hard or impossible even to ask the most important question, let alone to seek the evidence for answering it.

Nationalists claim to love their own culture in virtue of its particular qualities: it is, they claim, exceedingly beautiful. When they contemplate it, their feelings are deeply moved, and it is for this reason that they are patriots. Well and good: but if nationalism is a general phenomenon, covering a whole variety of nations, quite obviously it cannot be explained by the reasons operating internally within each national movement: these reasons must be specifically related to each nation and its culture; they cannot apply generally, otherwise there could hardly be *rival* nationalisms. So the general explanation cannot be internal to the cultures concerned: it must stand outside them and explain why, in general, culture*s* have become a political principle, a principle of the delimitation of political units. Whether cultures themselves are continuous or not is another question.

If the continuity of cultures is an open question, which probably has a diversity of specific answers rather than a single general one, what of the issue of the political sex-appeal of cultures, whether permanent or ephemeral? Here again, it is not clear that there is an exceptionless *general* answer. Some cultures have in the past inspired political action, but on the whole, this has been exceptional. In our modern world, nationalism is not the only force, nor is it always victorious. All we can say is this: we are in possession (and have offered) an inherently plausible and persuasive argument which purports to show (a) that homogeneity of culture is an unlikely determinant of political boundaries in the agrarian world, and a very probable one in the modern, industrial/scientific world, and (b) that the transition from

Agraria to Industria is also the transition from a world in which high (literacy and education-linked) cultures are a minority accomplishment and privilege (if they exist at all), to a world in which they become the pervasive culture of society as a whole. We have linked these general observations to the emergence of nationalism.

The available evidence fits *on the whole*, at any rate in Europe, but it doesn't fit perfectly and everywhere. There the matter rests, until further evidence is marshalled or further arguments presented. The counter-evidence and counter-arguments provided certainly do not warrant a repudiation of the theory, but equally, they do not justify the theory being treated as firmly established. If true, and that remains to be seen, it does link nationalism to the modern world, without prejudice to the occasional persistence of cultures over time, or the occasional power of cultures to inspire political action and loyalty in the past. For all that, if we are to understand nationalism, it seems to me that we must look above all at what is distinctive in the modern world, rather than at what it shares with the past. My own view is that some nations possess genuine ancient navels, some have navels invented for them by their own nationalist propaganda, and some are altogether navel-less. My belief is also that the middle category is by far the largest, but I stand open to correction by genuine research. At any rate, this is how the question should be formulated.

An example:
Czech nationalism

Czech nationalism is as good a test case as any. Czech culture and its relationship to a Prague-based polity is very neatly located halfway between navel-less nations, and nations possessed of what seem to be well-authenticated historic navels. The Estonians, for example, are a fine example of highly successful navel-free nationalism. At the beginning of the nineteenth century, they did not really exist as a self-conscious category: they could only refer to themselves as 'those who lived on the land', in distinction to Swedish or German burghers or Russian bureaucrats. There wasn't even an ethnonym.

However, just as the previously operative conditions of agrarian society permitted or favoured domination by a tiny alien minority, now the conditions of modern life favoured the demographic majority, however unfavourable its political baseline. A national culture was born, by the usual nineteenth-century methods (national theatre, museum, education). The process was brilliantly successful, and very thorough: the ethnographic museum in Tartu, for instance, has approximately one cultural object for every ten Estonians, and is sustained by a conscientious network of informants. Estonian culture is not in peril: rates of literacy, the level of education and general consciousness are extremely high. Political independence was secured on the collapse of the Tsarist empire and recovered on the collapse of the Bolshevik one. The fact that there is no historic precedent for a linkage of Estonian culture with a state does not matter in the least: this nationalism is so brazenly devoid of any navel that it does not even deign to invent one, and yet the national culture is so vigorous as to be in no danger at all, and the political will accompanying it is also strong and effective. (Note the interesting contrast with not so distant Byelorussia, which contests a navel with Luthania: was the powerful medieval Duchy of Lithuania 'really' Lithuanian or Byelorussian? Its point of origin was Lithuanian, but, it is claimed, the main language used was the Slav dialect which is the ancestor of modern Byelorussian. Here we have one navel, two nations.)

At the other extreme from Estonia, we have modern political units which clearly have political institutional ancestors, which in turn had a close connection with a high culture. The Czechs are in between. Medieval and early-modern Bohemia (and the other 'lands of the Crown of St Wenceslas') was indisputably an important political entity, with equally indisputable (though not clearly defined) links to a Czech culture and a written language with its own high culture. None of that is in dispute, at least in general outline. But in the seventeenth century, with the end of the wars of religion and the settlement of the Peace of Westphalia, the Bohemian kingdom in effect disappeared from the political map of Europe. At first, it survived nominally as one element in the Habsburg dominions, united with the others only through the monarch, by personal union, but even this nominal survival grew ever more shadowy. The larger successor unit ceased to have links to the Czech language, which lost its role as a vehicle of a high culture, and became largely a peasant dialect. However, with the demographic growth and social mobility induced by the industrial revolution, the Czech-speakers, constituting a majority in Bohemia and Moravia, gradually reconquered the cities and restored a high role to their language.

However, there is an important difference in comparison with the Estonians. The Estonians had no historic navel. They were born by a process of nation-formation under nationalism-favouring conditions, and they did not bother or could not manage, to invent one. Not so the Czechs: a navel was available, accessible to any competent historian. The Bohemian Kingdom was important, the University of Prague dated back to the fourteenth century, and its history even contained an unambigiously nationalist theme, the relative representation in the university of Czech and other students. But even more important than all this: in the early fifteenth century, a proto-Protestant movement, the Hussites, was based on Bohemia and successfully resisted Papal and Imperial attempts to suppress it. Here Bohemia and Czech culture made a significant contribution to European history.

The most important figure in the history of Czech nationalism was, of course, the president-liberator Tomas Masaryk, a university professor who succeeded in becoming a uniquely successful philosopher-king. It was almost as if, in Italy, Mazzini, Cavour and Garibaldi had all been one and the same person: Masaryk worked out the theory, carried out the international negotiations and commanded the Czech Legions during the First World War which were meant to underwrite or legitimise the claim to national independence.

What exactly was Masaryk's theory? It should be noted that Masaryk's writings are of genuine importance. They are not read simply because he was a political success. He was, above all, a moralist, rather than a romantic nationalist. He justified his nationalism because it made a contribution to the overall trend of history, which in turn was a profoundly moral one. The secret of history was the passage from authoritarian and dogmatic political and clerical systems, to liberal and democratic ones. The Czech bid for independence was justified by the fact that the Habsburgs had failed to liberate themselves from their traditional authoritarianism and Catholic dogmatism: it is for this reason that they had to be consigned to the dustheap of history. Spurred on by the opportunities offered by war, Masaryk abandoned the view of Palacky, the Czech historian-awakener, who had favoured 'Austro-Slavism': that is, a Danubian state which would group together the small nations of central Europe and protect them from German expansionism and Russian autocracy.

Note that Masaryk's highly moral nationalism had an internationalist major premise: it was the overall tendency of history towards freedom and democracy which vindicated Czech nationalism and independence as one of its instruments. It was not wilful, inward-looking nationalism. Quite the contrary.

However, for Masaryk, the Czecks were not Johnny-come-latelies of the universal democratic tendency. He enlisted the Hussites and the various sectarian movements which followed them as proto-democrats and egalitarians. Czech values had always pointed in the desirable direction, and only the unfortunate defeat of 1620 had, for three sad centuries, suppressed this benign tendency.

So Masaryk not merely led Czech nationalism to its victory in 1918 and its ratification at the Versailles settlement, but he also provided it with its navel. Now the question before us, as theoreticians of nationalism concerned with the primordialism–modernism debate, is this: was this navel genuine-historical, or invented?

For Masaryk, of course, it was genuine. He was aware of some evidence against the thesis of full continuity between fifteenth-century Czechs and modern ones. He deplored the movement towards greater subjection of the peasantry in the late fifteenth century, carried out by men who, on his own principal thesis, should have been the precursors of modern democracy. It was a regrettable lapse on their part.

For other Czechs, however, Masaryk was mistaken not on points of detail, but at the very heart of his thesis. During the suppression of liberty under Communism, the leadership of the only overt opposition movement, Charter 77, was taken over by another philosophy professor, Jan Patocka. In a remarkable and posthumously published book, Patocka recorded his own vision of Czech character, destiny and historic role. In some ways, he is only repeating or reapplying arguments of earlier critics of Masaryk, such as the highly influential historian Pekar.

The Patocka position consists of a repudiation of the navel postulated by Masaryk. In outline, the rival vision runs as follows: there is no continuity between the Hussites and the admittedly egalitarian and liberal modern Czech nation. All this is anachronism: the Hussites belonged to the Middle Ages and would not make good modern social democrats. The real roots of modern Czech culture lie in the reactions of a Catholic peasantry to the Enlightenment bureaucratic centralisation introduced by the Habsburgs in the late eighteenth century, a reaction perpetuated during the movement of that peasantry to the towns. Admittedly, when they needed a theory, they did turn to the rediscovered Hussites, whose egalitarianism provided a warrant for their own plebeian tendencies (Patocka disliked both). The Masarykian navel was spurious. A genuine one, of much less antiquity, was available. The genuine one (on the Pekar–Patocka view) had the additional disadvantage of contradicting the national myth of the Czechs as a valiant advance-guard of democracy in an otherwise benighted central Europe.

This disadvantage, in changed circumstances, could become an advantage. Masaryk had used his version of Czech history as a charter for a vehemently pro-western foreign policy: Czech democracy would be made safe by its alliance with the West, which was democratic and invincible, as history decreed. Democracy and the French army were invincible, if indeed the two could be distinguished.

Munich put paid to these illusions. The democratic West did not stand by its ideological acolytes, and 1940 proved that it was also very far from invincible. Munich destroyed Masaryk's philosophy of history. It did not destroy the Czech penchant for a democratic-egalitarian style of politics, and when democracy returned after the collapse of Communism, it no longer had a Masarykian flavour. We are democrats in virtue of our consumerism, not some highfalutin historical trend: western markets interest us more than western values. Little Czech-land-ism, especially after the successful shedding of the local Mezzogiorno, rather than philosophy of history, set the tone. When economic laissez-fairists and Catholics combined in the new government of the reduced and inward-turned Czech Republic, Patocka's navel (not a perfect fit either) was probably closer to them than Masaryk's.

Some nations have navels, some achieve navels, some have navels thrust upon them. Those possessed of genuine ones are probably in a minority, but it matters little. It is the need for navels engendered by modernity that matters.

SIXTEEN

Practical implications

Nationalist conflict has caused enormous suffering, both directly and indirectly. Nationalism is not just a phenomenon, it is also a problem, and not only for those who, through commitment to either internationalism or a class-based theory of legitimacy, hold nations to be an inherently improper foundation of the political order. Even if one is not committed a priori to some definite theory concerning the proper constitution or delimitation of the state, one must still be perturbed by the havoc, suffering, cruelty and injustice often brought by nationalism. Does the present theory, if valid, carry any practical implications or recommendations concerning how this problem should be handled?

There is no magic formula for calming ethnic conflict and replacing it with sweetness and light. It does certainly follow from the account offered that it is fairly pointless simply to indulge in moralistic preaching against nationalism, invoking the brotherhood of all men. The impulsion towards nationalist sentiment in politics has, in our view, exceedingly profound roots in the lifestyle of modern man, which makes for homogeneity of a single high culture within any one political unit, and which condemns those not masters of the said culture, or unacceptable within it, to a humiliating, painful second-class status. This situation cannot but make men into nationalists, and it is better to try and deal with the conditions which engender nationalism than to preach at its victims and beg them to refrain from feeling what, in their circumstances, it is only too natural to feel.

At the same time, it is misguided to see nationalism as a consequence of some universal territorial or kin drive. Men may or may not, in some measure, be under the sway of dark gods and obtain their satisfaction from indulging those deities, and what those deities require may not be pleasant to behold. This is also a problem we must face, and its manifestations may well overlap with the problem which concerns us here. Civilisation may always have its discontents, and we may be doomed to a painful compromise between instinctual satisfaction and civilised living, and also between the longing for a gratifying, 'meaningful' order and the demands of rationality and scepticism. Disenchantment, alienation, anomie, the Iron Cage, all these may be our lot, and the social order may need to recognise them rather than aspire to abolish them. But the problem of nationalism is more specific and should not be identified with these wider forms of anguish. It calls for a more specific diagnosis and more specific remedies or palliatives.

What are they?

Political stability is in itself a good. This much is right in conservatism. The idea that any ongoing, established political order deserves to be corrected, or even abolished, because it fails to satisfy an abstract principle (such as the 'self-determination of nations'), is indeed absurd – as absurd as the contrary supposition that the sheer existence of a power structure, of a political system, automatically confers legitimacy on it. Some 'really existing' systems (to adapt the pathetic final attempt of Bolshevism to claim legitimacy in virtue of its real existence, not destined, as it happens, to last very long) really are not viable, and the correct question, in their case, is not whether, but how to change and replace them. In our age, many political systems which combined cultural pluralism with a persisting inequality between the cultures concerned fall into this class. They are doomed, in virtue of their violation of the nationalist principle which, in past ages, could be violated with impunity.

In general (though no absolute rules can be postulated), political systems should be abrogated or changed slowly rather than abruptly. It was naive to express unqualified joy at the sudden dissolution of (say) the Habsburg, Soviet or Yugoslav states. Conservatives are right to this extent: the most effective social cement is continuity, custom and the consensus based not on reason (there seldom are any good reasons for obeying this rather than that authority): people obey established authorities and observe established customs and procedures because others do so as well. By joining the silent majority, any particular individual or group increases the prospect of peace and the possibility of getting on with its own business undisturbed. Once the established order is disturbed, however, it is not clear where legitimacy and authority lie, and the rival claimants can only prevail not by good reasons, but by greater terror. It is no accident that so many ideological revolutions end in terror, and so many dissolutions of empire in internecine and bloody warfare.

It must always be borne in mind that, generally speaking, there are *no* solutions or answers in ethnic confrontations. Some solutions may be conspicuously more unjust than others, but there are *no* just ones. 'The right of nations to self-determination' *sounds* like a principle which could be implemented, and generate unique and hence uniquely binding solutions in diverse concrete conflict situations. But this is rubbish. Various procedures involved in applying the idea cut across each other: is it demography, history or geography which is to prevail? The application of the demographic principle (let the majority of the population be heard and be decisive) depends on how the electoral units are drawn, and this demarcation can easily be manipulated to render diverse answers. There is the not insignificant consideration of safety and security: our nation has been attacked before and probably will be attacked again, so can we tolerate a boundary which enables the enemy to cut the country in half with ease, or to shell the capital with even small guns? There is the piquant principle invoked in Kosovo: can a nation be expected to separate itself from a piece of land which witnessed its greatest national disaster, even if that land is now largely inhabited by aliens?

No electoral units are dictated; they are chosen by us, and the answer depends on how they are chosen. Is historic continuity or geographic coherence to be ignored? There is also the principle that even a cultural/national group which is not in a majority *anywhere* may nevertheless, or all the more, require to have a safe haven, shelter, base, somewhere. There is also the fact that the involvement of a culture with a territory differs according to whether the population in question produced microchips, grew potatoes, herded camels or hunted reindeer. Industrial populations move rapidly and cannot be said to mix their life with the soil in any intimate way: one industrial suburb is much like any other; location matters little. For obvious reasons, agrarian populations are more closely linked to the soil, though they may not care for it so much. Pastoral populations know intimately the land they use, but they wander far afield. So do hunters, but they tend to be very small in numbers, and in modern conditions they are almost always swamped numerically by alien immigrants. So is one to propose a formula that, for the territorial claims by groups seeking self-determination (held to be impossible without sovereignty over territory), one hunter equals five pastoralists or ten agriculturalists or a hundred industrial workers? Are industrial workers an inferior form of humanity, then? Are they not capable, on occasion, of a deep and sincere love for their native land? Being more often literate than the other categories, they are more likely to be familiar with romantic literature, and may actually have these sentiments more often.

In brief: the various criteria are almost always in conflict. So 'solutions' can never be based on justice alone, for justice in this matter is not one but many. Given that this is so, the extraneous factors which *must* intrude ('justice' not providing a uniquely determined answer) should include the consideration of stability and continuity. The status quo is not sacrosanct, but it should be treated with respect, though not reverence. The idea that the real is the rational is one of the greatest imbecilities ever asserted in philosophy (though there are other claimants to this title). The weaker idea, that the real may have some merit, may be less bad than some alternatives, and ought not to be discarded without some due and deliberate process – that idea should be taken seriously.

Next to stability and continuity comes affluence. People who are affluent and, above all, who believe themselves to be in a situation which will fairly soon improve and continue to do so are much less likely to be tempted into violent conduct which will disrupt their world, than people whose situation is deteriorating and looks like continuing to do so – let alone people whose situation is desperate. Apart from this general consideration, which perhaps applies to all men, there are the specific consequences of industrial affluence, which softens manners and makes men less tolerant of the discomforts, hardships and dangers of violent conflict. Citizens of socially and economically very advanced countries seldom make very good or eager soldiers.

Advanced industrialism may well lead, simultaneously, to greater ultimate political units, and to greater local autonomy: to what might be called cantonisation. Effective supranational authority may be dictated by the general development of technology: the resources required for the production of devastating nuclear, biological or other weapons are growing smaller and smaller. The know-how required for their production is inevitably becoming ever more widely available. The time cannot be far off when only effective central control can avert either ecological catastrophe or the use of effective blackmail by small groups willing and able to impose terrible punishment on those not complying with their dictates. This would seem to be the argument for the eventual inevitability of a supranational authority, which alone could handle these dangers.

At the same time, however, a different tendency is also operative. The enjoyment of industrial affluence depends only in part on the possessions of individuals and families; it depends, at least as much, on a lumpy infrastructure which cannot be erected or maintained individually. Consequence: a very high proportion of the global product passes not through individual, but through collective/political hands, which administer the said infrastructure. This in turn has a further consequence: it is very much in the interest of all possible interest groups to organise and mobilise, and try to influence the deployment of, that collectively run part of the state in their own interest. Among these potential interest groups, regional ones are the most obvious ones, and there are indeed signs of their greater vitality and self-assertion.

If these two trends are really in operation, the consequence may eventually be that the advanced industrial world will once again, like the agrarian world of the past, be one in which effective political units will be either larger or smaller than 'national' units based on similarity of high culture. Just as, once upon a time, city-states were sub-ethnic and empires were super-ethnic, so the agencies preventing nuclear and ecological disaster, controlling the drugs and arms trades, and so on, will have to be super-ethnic, while the agency administering the school and welfare system may become sub-ethnic. This is a hope rather than a prediction, but it is not an unreasonable hope.

Finally, there is the development of non-territorial cultural associations, which would in some measure separate patriotism (love of one's culture and its carriers) from obsession with territory. Our century has witnessed one successful de-territorialisation of nationalism: everyone knows now that the power and prestige of a nation depends on its annual rate of growth and its economic clout, and *not* on how much of the map it manages to paint with its own colour. A further de-territorialisation, the capacity to love, say,

Ruritanian folk music without absolutely insisting on exclusive sovereignty over the villages in which that music was allegedly first sung, would be eminently desirable. But it will be exceedingly difficult: the entire weight of romantic literature is on the side of fetishisation of landscape, of national culture as expressed in land-use and in its territorial delimitation. On the other hand, modern communication technology should make it possible for two or more national TV networks to be equally accessible in the same 'land' ... Anyway: in those very extensive parts of the globe where there is a great proliferation of cultures, there are only two possibilities: either such pluralism, de-fetishisation of land, will be achieved, or there has to be ethnic cleansing. A humane person can hardly have any hesitation in making his choice.

These are the only general recommendations one can make: a preference for stability, an avoidance of destabilisation without strong cause and without provision for an orderly passage to a successor regime; affluence; centralisation of major order-maintaining functions and a cantonisation of social ones; cultural pluralism, de-fetishisation of land. These recommendations may be banal, but they are at least set in the context of a coherent overall theory of what constitutes the problem. If anyone knows of better recommendations which are at the same time realistic, I shall be only too glad to hear about them.

⹋REFERENCES

Cruise O'Brien, C. (1988) *God Land: Reflections on Religion and Nationalism*. London: Harvard University Press.

Hobsbawm, E. and T. Ranger (1983) *The Invention of Tradition*. Cambridge: Cambridge University Press.

Kedourie, E. (1993) [1960]. *Nationalism* (4th expanded edition). Oxford: Blackwell.

Lenski, G. (1966) *Power and Privilege: A Theory of Social Stratification*. New York: McGraw-Hill.

Mach, Z. (1985) 'National symbols in the context of ritual: the Polish example', *Journal of the Anthropological Society of Oxford*, 16: 19–34.

Mann, M. (1992) 'The emergence of modern European nationalism', in J. A. Hall and I. C. Jarvie (eds), *Transition to Modernity: Essays on Power, Wealth and Belief*. Cambridge: Cambridge University Press.

Plamenatz, J. (1973) 'Two types of nationalism', in E. Kamenka (ed.), *Nationalism: The Nature and Evolution of an Idea*. London: Edward Arnold.

Szporluk, K. R. (1988) *Communism and Nationalism: Karl Marx versus Friedrich List*. New York: Oxford University Press.

Turner, B. (1974) *Weber and Islam: A Critical Study*. London: Routledge and Kegan Paul.

Zubaida, S. (1995) 'Is there a Muslim society? Ernest Gellner's sociology of Islam', *Economy and Society*, 24: 151–81.

≡INDEX